Kathryn Kuhlman, a Theology of Miracles

Kathryn Kuhlman, a Theology of Miracles

DR. MARGARET DE ALMINANA

BRIDGE LOGOS

Newberry, FL 32669

Bridge-Logos
Newberry, FL 32669

Kathryn Kuhlman, a Theology of Miracles: Understanding Spiritual Encounter
by Dr. Margaret English de Alminana

Printed in the United States of America.

Library of Congress Catalog Card Number: 2020949847

International Standard Book Number: 978-1-61036-255-9

Cover/Interior design by Kent Jensen | knail.com

Dedication

To students of the Holy Spirit and all of those
who continue to wait on God for your healing,
this book is written for you.

Table of Contents

CHAPTER ONE

Introduction—A One-Woman Healing Fountain

Kathryn Kuhlman (1907–1976) oversaw one of the most expansive ministries in the 20th century, drawing massive crowds wherever she went, pilgrims who would camp outside in all weather for days to attend her meetings. Widely popular for stunning miracles that accompanied her services, the press called her a "one woman Fountain of Lourdes."[1] The title originated from a *Time Magazine* article in 1970, and her attendees—an eclectic collection of rough factory workers, Catholic priests and nuns, hippies and celebrities, both saved and sinner together—considered it a title of honor.[2] Kathryn Kuhlman's ministry was a

1 Considered by Roman Catholics as one of the most important mystical wonders of modern times, the Fountain of Lourdes resides in a little town in the South of France. Roman Catholic pilgrims travel from around the globe to seek healings at the waters, which they believe hold curative powers.

2 Jamie Buckingham, *Daughter of Destiny*, (Newberry, FL: Bridge-Logos, 1999), 224.

total departure from the popular healing ministries that preceded her. Completely unique, she set an expectation and a pace for generations of both healers and seekers to follow. Few did so, however, with a full grasp of her unique theological perspective as well as her embodied practical theory, or praxis, which she developed thoughtfully and intentionally over time and operated in with scrupulous care and attention to detail.

Possibly thousands attested to having been healed in her services, but the great gatherings of people were offered even more. For many did not come for healing but to encounter for themselves the unique and powerful Divine Presence experienced at her meetings.

A HEALING OF LYMPHOMA

Although it is not the intention of this book to argue the veracity of the thousands of testimonies of healing that would follow the Kuhlman ministry, this work will include one medically documented account from the 1977, June 12 edition of *The Pentecostal Evangel.*[3] In it Robert L. Bayles shares the events surrounding his wife, Rachel Bayles's, experiences with lymphoma and her subsequent healing during a Kathryn Kuhlman service at Los Angeles in February 24, 1974.

> In late January 1972 my wife Rachel discovered a growing lump on the left side of her neck. There was another one over the collarbone on the same side. Our family doctor scheduled an operation to find the cause and nature of

3 L. Bayles, "Minister's Wife Healed of Lymphoma," *The Pentecostal Evangel*, (June 12, 1977), 21.

the lumps. They proved to be malignant; the disease was diagnosed as lymphosarcoma or lymphoma. X-rays showed there were also tumors in the chest and large ones in front of each kidney.[4]

Ms. Bayles underwent 28 cobalt treatments for the neck and chest and was scheduled for similar treatments for the abdomen. But because she was extremely ill and was hospitalized for negative effects of the treatments, the Southern California Superintendent of the Assemblies of God made funds available to place Bayles in the Beverly Hills Doctor's Hospital in Los Angeles, where she spent 107 days. Twice during the stay Rev. Bayles was called to her bedside because doctors feared her imminent death.

Released from the hospital on September 1, 1972, she continued chemotherapy treatments until February 1974, when the couple was informed that the tumors had begun to grow again. Several days later, though she was weak and wheelchair bound, Bayles took his wife to a Kuhlman service.

Rachel Bayles began to tremble during the service and swelling from phlebitis in her leg receded. Kuhlman called her to the platform and prayed for her. A few weeks later, doctors took another set of x-rays and found that the tumors had vanished. She stopped taking her medicine and when she returned to the hospital for scans and x-rays, she was informed that her lymph system had returned to normal. On October 6, 1975, Rachel Bayles's doctor declared her cured.[5]

---

4 Ronald L. Bayles, "Minister's Wife Healed of Lymphoma." 21.

5 Ronald L. Bayles, "Minister's Wife Healed of Lymphoma." 21.

Customarily at Kuhlman services, the evangelist formed neither healing lines for seekers nor did she lay her hands on their heads. Instead, she simply declared that a healing was taking place in the seating area where a particular seeker was located, a method some called a *word of knowledge* or using divinely imparted information regarding the Holy Spirit's healing activity.

AN UNUSUALLY TOUCHED LIFE

In the 1970s, believers and skeptics alike acknowledged that her life was unusually touched by a spiritual presence. In 1976, a *New York Times* obituary declared: "Kathryn Kuhlman, regarded by devotees and doubters alike as one of America's most popular evangelists and faith healers, died Friday at Hillcrest Medical Center in Tulsa, Okla, where she had been since undergoing open-heart surgery on Dec. 28. … For more than a quarter century, Miss Kuhlman crisscrossed the nation, holding prayer and healing sessions and inducing 'miracles,' which she attributed to God, but which skeptics labeled psychosomatic."[6]

Kuhlman (1907–1976) held regular services attended by thousands in Los Angeles, Pittsburgh, Oakland, Miami, Chicago, and in other major cities throughout the U.S. and Canada. She also held meetings in Sweden in 1974 and in Jerusalem in 1974 (where this researcher had the privilege of attending) and again in 1975.[7] Weekly television shows were broadcast throughout the

6 Gary Settle, (February 22, 1976). "Kathryn Kuhlman, Evangelist And Faith Healer, Dies in Tulsa." *New York Times.* Retrieved 2020-6-15.

7 Kathryn Kuhlman, Curriculum Vitae provided by Carol Gray, executive director of the Kathryn Kuhlman Foundation, 4411 Stilley Road, Brentwood, PA., 11/19/2010, 2.

United States and Canada for more than a decade until her death in 1976; 490 half-hour shows were televised by CBS Television in Los Angles. Fifty radio stations carried her 30-minute broadcasts, five days a week, covering most of the U.S. and Canada. Overseas broadcasts reached much of Europe.[8] Newspapers around the world carried her name, and even *Laugh-In*'s Ruth Buzzi hammed her gestures and voice, in an act that Kuhlman enjoyed and responded to with a letter and a gift of flowers.[9]

As an author, Kuhlman produced three full-length, hardcover books published by Prentice-Hall and later released in paperback by Pyramid, and republished by Bridge Publishing[10] in 1992 and 1993. Books she authored include: *I Believe in Miracles,* (1962), which sold more than 2 million copies; *God Can Do It Again,* (1969), *Nothing Is Impossible with God,* (1974). She also authored seven companion books published through Bethany Fellowship.[11]

She never built a building or erected a church but, through the Kathryn Kuhlman Foundation, she made numerous charitable donations to ministries and missions, including college scholarships to Wheaton College, Cincinnati Conservatory of Music, National Medical College in Hong Kong, Evangel College, in Springfield, MO, Kent State University, Carnegie Mellon University, and Oral Roberts University, among others.[12]

---

8 Kathryn Kuhlman, Curriculum Vitae provided by Carol Gray.

9 Jamie Buckingham, *Daughter of Destiny* (Newberry, FL: Bridge-Logos, 1999) 181-182.

10 The company was renamed Bridge-Logos Publishing after Bridge merged with Logos International.

11 Kathryn Kuhlman, Curriculum Vitae provided by Carol Gray, executive director of the Kathryn Kuhlman Foundation, 4411 Stilley Road, Brentwood, PA., 11/19/2010, 2.

12 Kathryn Kuhlman, Curriculum Vitae provided by Carol Gray, 3.

THE KATHRYN KUHLMAN FOUNDATION

The Kathryn Kuhlman Foundation, begun in 1954, was formed as a "religious, charitable, non-profit organization" that continued to provide help to numerous ministry outreaches around the world for many years after her death. Its stated purpose was characteristically non-sectarian: "To promote, foster and interpret Christianity to the world and engage in other religious and charitable and educational activities."[13] Although largely unsung, the multi-focused endeavor fulfilled its purposes well. Twenty-four mission stations were erected overseas wholly financed by the foundation. The KKF boasts that "each station was presented debt-free to the native people as a gift."[14] The foreign missions sites created are listed as follows:

- Corn Island, Nicaragua, Central America
- Boaco, Nicaragua, Central America
- Waspam, Nicaragua, Central America
- Choluteca, Honduras, Central America
- San Isidro, Costa Rica
- Esteli, Nicaragua, Central America
- Thakurpukur, India
- Macau
- Hong Kong Roof Top School
- Cotonou, Dahomey, West Africa

13 "Kathryn Kuhlman: A Legacy" (Pittsburgh, PA: The Kathryn Kuhlman Foundation, n.d.) back cover. See also, Warner, Wayne E., "At the Grass-Roots: Kathryn Kuhlman's Pentecostal-Charismatic Influence on Historic Mainstream Churches," *Pneuma: The Journal of the Society for Pentecostal Studies*, (Vol. 17., No. 1, Spring 1995), 51-65, 51.

14 Kathryn Kuhlman, Curriculum Vitae provided by Carol Gray, executive director of the Kathryn Kuhlman Foundation, 4411 Stilley Road, Brentwood, PA., 11/19/2010.

- Mar de Plata, Argentina, South America
- Santa Lucia, Nicaragua, Central America
- Taipai, Formosa
- Pretoria, Republic of South Africa
- Johannesburg, Republic of South Africa
- Rustenburg, South Africa
- East London, South Africa
- Kuala Lumpur, Malaysia
- Surabaja, Indonesia
- Viet Nam Chapel, (Tin Lanh Military Chapel)
- Ranger Clinic, Saigon, Viet Nam
- Bible School Reconstruction, Managua, Nicaragua, Central America
- Kathryn Kuhlman Memorial Church, Nairobi, East Africa
- Kathryn Kuhlman Memorial Church, El Salvador, Central America[15]

The Ranger Clinic in Saigon was built and fully equipped with funds supplied by the Kathryn Kuhlman Foundation. A specially trained nurse was retained to attend to the paraplegics and amputees at the expense of the foundation as well.[16] In addition to funding missions overseas, the Kuhlman Foundation helped to underwrite Teen Challenge, directed by David Wilkerson, a recovery ministry for drug addicted teenagers and young adults. "She personally raised and gave to Teen Challenge the money to build a place on our farm to reach and rehabilitate hopeless addicts."[17]

15 Kathryn Kuhlman, Curriculum Vitae, 2.

16 Kathryn Kuhlman, Curriculum Vitae, 2.

17 Wayne Warner, *Kathryn Kuhlman: The Woman Behind the Miracles* (Ann Arbor, MI: Servant Pub., 1993), 196.

David Wilkerson, author of *The Cross and the Switchblade,*[18] and founder of Teen Challenge, described Kuhlman's ministry as one driven by a deep, genuine, and unfettered compassion for the poor and needy. He said,

> She is not wealthy, nor is she hung up on materialism. I know! She personally raised and gave to Teen Challenge the money to build a place on our farm to reach and rehabilitate hopeless addicts. Her prayers have brought in the money to build churches in underdeveloped countries around the world. She has sponsored the educating of underprivileged children and other talented youth who were recipients of her love and concern. She has walked with me into the ghettos of New York and laid loving hands on filthy addicts. She never winced or withdrew—her concern was genuine.[19]

"Recognizing her ability to raise funds to be used for reaching others with the gospel, Kuhlman put much of the money back into her media ministry and the overseas effort of the Assemblies of God and the Christian Missionary Alliance. In 1972 alone the Foundation gave almost $500,000 to several missions projects in the United States and overseas."[20] Adjusted for inflation, the amount in today's dollars would be $3,126,204.38.[21]

18 David Wilkerson, *The Cross and the Switchblade,* (NYC: Penguin Putnam, Inc., 1962).

19 Kathryn Kuhlman, *Nothing Is Impossible with God,* (Englewood Cliffs, New Jersey: Prentice-Hall, Inc., 1974), vi.

20 Wayne E. Warner, *Kathryn Kuhlman: The Woman Behind the Miracles* (Ann Arbor, MI: Servant Pub., 1993) 200; see also, Buckingham, *Daughter of Destiny,* 208.

21 "Dollar Times Inflation Index: https://www.dollartimes.com/inflation/inflation.php?amount=500000&year=1972. 6/18/20.

In addition to the formal charitable work of the Foundation, Kuhlman and her staff gathered funds, toys, clothing and much more in amounts too vast to recall to help meet the endless needs she uncovered through her correspondence ministry and religious services. Viola Malachuck, a personal friend, recalled that the basement of her modest, suburban Pittsburgh home, located in Fox Chapel, PA, was filled with toys she gathered for children for Christmas. Beyond the grueling media and service schedules, Kuhlman worked tirelessly behind the scenes in what amounted to a ceaseless outpouring of philanthropic work.

The vast and tireless charitable work is one of the most notable features of Kuhlman's life, although it was unpublicized. Another interesting and notable feature of her ministry is that she, together with a very small staff, personally responded to every letter the ministry received. Biographer Jamie Buckingham notes that the staff often slept on couches in her ministry offices, which were piled high with letters, boxes, and gifts and were continually abuzz with the ceaseless activity of this concern. If it is in the small things that an individual distinguishes him or herself, Kuhlman did so with the writing of letters of encouragement to those seeking healing, condolences for the bereaved, and faith and optimism for those encountering various struggles. Although she seemed a larger-than-life figure on television and radio and in her massive services, Kuhlman remained surprisingly approachable to the end through the mail.

Kuhlman was awarded an honorary Doctor of Humane Letters degree from Oral Roberts University on May 28, 1972. She was named in "Who's Who in California" 39th Edition in 1975.

The Speaker of the House, Carl Albert, presented Kuhlman with the flag flown over the Capitol Building in Washington, D.C., commemorating her twenty-five years of preaching in Pittsburgh, in 1972. She was presented keys to Pittsburgh, Los Angeles, and St. Louis by their representative mayors. Beyond these notable honors, Kuhlman was given a private audience with Pope John Paul in Oct. 11, 1972, where he affirmed her "admirable work" and gave her his blessing.[22]

Although a towering figure, something about Kuhlman always seemed approachable and familiar. She touched multitudes, but she never lost touch with her humble roots.

22 Kathryn Kuhlman, Curriculum Vitae provided by Carol Gray, 1.

CHAPTER TWO

Biographical Sketch—A Look at the Life of Kathryn Kuhlman

As a young girl of but 16 tender years, Kathryn Kuhlman left her farming community of Concordia, MO, in 1924, to travel the nation as a tent ministry helper. Her sister, Myrtle, had married a successful Pentecostal evangelist with a traveling tent ministry named Everett Parrott. Newspaper clips announced the booming ministry as featuring a 200-voice choir and a 50-piece orchestra. "Past Parrott revival meetings are said to have attracted crowds numbering as high as 6,000 persons for a single service."[23]

The roaring twenties were highlighted by celebrities, including the famed evangelist Aimee Semple McPherson, who

23 "Rev. Parrott Will Open Revival Campaign Here: First Meeting Sunday, 200 voices, 50-Piece Orchestra, To Assist at All Services," newspaper article (n.d.). Provided by the Flower Center.

notoriously ruled the headlines with both sensation and scandal. Although Kuhlman herself disavowed any link whatsoever to the celebrated female evangelist of the 1920s and 30s, a direct link was established by historian Wayne Warner. Kuhlman left Missouri in 1924[24] to join her sister and brother-in-law in ministry as itinerant tent revivalist,[25] but it was hitherto undiscovered that she had attended Aimee Semple McPherson's Bible School, the Lighthouse of International Foursquare Evangelism in Los Angeles, in addition to studying at the Simpson Bible Institute (C&MA) in Seattle in those early years.[26]

According to Warner, Kuhlman quit high school in 1924[27] to follow her sister and brother-in-law as they led revivals up and down the West Coast. During those years she also attended Simpson Bible Institute, a small Seattle school run by the Christian and Missionary Alliance. Later she enrolled in night classes at Aimee Semple McPherson's Bible school, Lighthouse of International Foursquare Evangelism in Los Angeles. Kuhlman never acknowledged these educational experiences, always insisting that the Holy Spirit was her only teacher.[28]

---

24 Buckingham dates this event as having occurred in 1923. See Jamie Buckingham, *Daughter of Destiny*, (South Plainfield, NJ: Bridge Publishing, 1976), 62.

25 Wayne E. Warner, *Kathryn Kuhlman: The Woman Behind the Miracles*, (Servant, 1993), 22.

26 Wayne E. Warner, *Kathryn Kuhlman*, (Ann Arbor, MI: Servant, 1993),34.

27 Some sources amend this disputed description of Kuhlman as having dropped out of high school by clarifying the information regarding the school system she attended in Concordia, MO, which has been said did not offer high school classes beyond the tenth grade.

28 Barbara Brown Zikmund, "A gift of healing," *Christian Century*, Aug. 2-9, 1995, 749.

Her resistance to the public's linking her ministry to McPherson's started early in her career. In 1933, at the height of the Great Depression, the young, itinerant evangelist launched a successful ministry in Denver. "Unfortunately, many of the people began to identify Kathryn with Aimee Semple McPherson, the flashy Pentecostal preacher from Los Angeles. Sister Aimee, as her followers called her, built her five-thousand seat Angeles Temple in Los Angles in 1923—the year Kathryn left home to join the Parrotts on the West Coast."[29] Everett Parrott had married Kathryn's sister, Myrtle, and the two traveled throughout the Northwest preaching the gospel from town to town. Kuhlman's ministry grew up in the midst of the McPherson scandal, which rocked the nation, and doubtless she found it expedient to create some distance between her fledgling upstart as controversies swirled around McPherson's ministry.

In the early days of Kuhlman's itinerant ministry, much of the nation offered a warm and welcoming embrace to the Pentecostal ministries of women. Although far from unbridled acceptance, a female minister could expect to gather a receptive crowd, and numerous churches continued to be headed by women throughout the nation, particularly in the Bible belt regions where Pentecostalism made significant inroads. "Women were effectively mobilized into service as ministers and founders during the early days of the Pentecostal movement both in North America and elsewhere, and the ministry of Pentecostal women continues today in many parts of the world."[30]

---

29 Buckingham, *Daughter of Destiny*, 62.

30 Allan Anderson, *An Introduction to Pentecostalism*, (Cambridge, UK: Cambridge University Press, 2004), 274.

Kuhlman denied ever having met McPherson. During a giant miracle service at the Angeles Temple years later in 1968, she told a crowd that she never met her. As close as she came was a visit to her grave some twenty years after she died.[31] She said, "I never met her. But several years ago, Maggie Hartner and I visited her grave. There we found a young man and a woman, who was probably his mother, viewing the monument erected to the memory of Miss McPherson. The woman was telling how her preaching had made Jesus so real. 'I found Christ through her life,' the woman said. Stirred, Kuhlman said, "If just one person can stand by my grave and say, 'I found Christ because she preached the gospel,' then I will not have lived in vain."[32]

McPherson offered upstart female preachers a double-edged sword. She and countless other Pentecostal pioneers opened the door through their tireless work, but the overspill of scandal tended to draw suspicion against them as well. Nevertheless, unlike female ministers today who might find crowds and venues unreceptive to them, Kuhlman seemed to experience little resistance. "'Name any little town in the state of Idaho,' Kathryn later told reporters, "and I worked at trying to evangelize it.'"[33]

THE EARLY DAYS

Kathryn Johanna Kuhlman (1907–1976) was born in Johnson County, near Concordia, MO. In an agrarian time, she was from pioneering stock, although her family would leave the 160-acre

31 Jamie Buckingham, *Daughter of Destiny*, (South Plainfield, NJ: Bridge Publishing, 1976), 62.

32 Jamie Buckingham, *Daughter of Destiny*, 63.

33 Jamie Buckingham, *Daughter of Destiny*, 47.

farm and move into the tiny town of Concordia shortly following her birth. Concordia was a German farming community located about sixty miles east of Kansas City. Kathryn was the third child born to Joseph A. Kuhlman and Emma Hader Walkenhorst. Joseph's mother, Katherine Marie Borgstadt, 1851–1907, after whom Kathryn was named, was born in Westphalia, Germany.[34] Grandmother had passed away just three months before daughter-in-law gave birth to baby Kathryn. Eldest daughter, Myrtle, was 15-years old when Kathryn was born, followed by 10-year-old brother Earl, who was called "Kooley"[35] and "Boy"[36] by the family, with Kathryn as next to the youngest in birth order, followed by Geneva nine years later.[37] As an adult looking back, the often playful Kuhlman would quip that her aunt begged the family not to name her Kathryn, protesting that "every mule in the state of Missouri is called Kate."[38]

Two years after Kathryn's birth Joseph Kuhlman purchased a large lot in town for $650, as recorded at the Lafayette County Court House. In 1911, the family, toting four-year-old Kathryn, moved in. The hard-working Kuhlmans lived there happily, and Joseph went into the dray business, operating the livery stable and running a delivery service. He became known as the wealthiest citizen in the lower middle-class community. And

34 Death certificates of Joseph A. Kuhlman, dated 12/30/34 and Emma Kuhlman dated 4/8/57, Missouri State Board of Health, Bureau of Vital Statistics.

35 Buckingham, *Daughter of Destiny,* 11.

36 Kathryn Kuhlman, "Strength for Thy Labor," Kathryn Kuhlman Foundation, #716, 1978, audiocassette.

37 Kathryn Kuhlman, *In Search of Blessing, Sermons on the Beatitudes,* (Alachua, FL: Bridge-Logos, 1989), 17, photo caption.

38 Kathryn Kuhlman, "An Hour with Kathryn Kuhlman," Kathryn Kuhlman Foundation, n.d. audiocassette.

even though he was a backslidden Baptist who refused to attend church, and according to his daughter would cross the street to avoid and oncoming pastor's invitation, he became the Lutheran community's mayor.[39]

Although she was well brought up, relatively speaking, she often described herself in terms that displayed a deep sense of personal humility. "I have nothing to offer," she would say. "I'm not pretty, I haven't got any talent, and I wouldn't cross the street to hear myself speak. I wasn't even born with hair on my head, just red fuzz."[40]

Years later, Kuhlman lamented in one of her daily radio talks that her brother "Boy," after an attack of appendicitis early in life—an often fatal condition in the early 1900s—was coddled and protected until he eventually lacked "gumption."[41] Folks in the community thought he was spoiled and "wild."[42]

Kathryn was known for having a wild streak of her own. She laughingly described herself as the kind of child who went on a hayride with the community's children, but was the only one who returned driving the cart.[43] On another occasion, she described a prank that she, as a child, played on her mother. As a structured, hard-working German, "Mama" religiously held to a weekly wash day schedule. Washing on Mondays was "part of her

---

39 Jamie Buckingham, *Daughter of Destiny*, (South Plainfield, NJ: Bridge Publishing, 1976), 14.

40 Kathryn Kuhlman, "Beginning of Miracles," Kathryn Kuhlman Foundation, K832, n.d., audiocassette.

41 Kathryn Kuhlman, "Faith," Kathryn Kuhlman Foundation, T5 #212, c. 1950s. Radio talk, audiocassette.

42 Buckingham, *Daughter of Destiny*, 15.

43 Kathryn Kuhlman, "An Hour with Kathryn Kuhlman," Kathryn Kuhlman Foundation, n.d., audio recording.

theology."[44] On that day, the entire house would be turned upside-down in a grand laundering production. Rigid and stern, Mama Kuhlman was the disciplinarian, while Joseph played more the role of a doting Grandpa than father.

Little Kathryn ran through the neighborhood announcing that it was her mother's birthday, asking the neighborhood's matrons to dress up for a party and to bring a cake. Having labored over boiling water, scrubbing clothes on washboards in galvanized tubes and hanging them on a line, Mama, with curlers in her hair, looking disheveled from the steaming ritual conducted in Missouri's stifling August heat, was awakened from a brief nap by a lineup of Concordia's social elite, all dressed in their Sunday best and bearing a cake. Mama was aghast, and young Kathryn spent a considerable amount of time in the basement, standing up, because of the spanking she received.[45]

The Kuhlman parents held polar opposite perspectives concerning their young daughter. "Joe Kuhlman might have told you what a generous little thing his red-haired girl was. To prove it he would tell you that while Mama attended a Methodist State Convention out of town, his six-year-old girl made iced tea for the whole neighborhood in Concordia, Missouri, delivering it to their back doors in gallon buckets, with Mama's compliments. ...this same wonderful red-haired girl of his, at the very height of watermelon season, plugged all of Grandpa's wonderful watermelons."[46] Later, Kuhlman confessed that she wanted to

44 Buckingham, *Daughter of Destiny*, 16.

45 Kathryn Kuhlman, "Why Was I Born? " Kathryn Kuhlman Foundation, #505, 1978. radio talk.

46 Kathryn Kuhlman, *Heart to Heart*, Vol. I, (Alachua, FL: Bridge-Logos, 1983), 76.

know that *all* of them were red inside, in order to confirm what her Grandfather Walkenhorst had explained.

SALVATION

When Kuhlman was six years old, elder sibling, Myrtle, married a student evangelist from the Assemblies of God, Everett B. Parrott, an event that would change the course of Kuhlman's life. Myrtle and Parrott moved to Chicago three years before the youngest daughter, Geneva, was born to Joseph and Emma.

In time, the town merchants came to know Kathryn as "little Joe," so often did she accompany him as he collected bills and made rounds.[47] Joseph was an astute businessman, and he taught his red-haired daughter the trade, imparting the business acumen she would use to great advantage later on when she would oversee one of the largest Pentecostal/Charismatic ministries of her time. Joseph was virtually unchurched, except for an occasional holiday service or special event involving his daughter. The spiritual leadership in the family fell to Emma, a staunch Methodist during a time when the Methodist tradition still retained some of its early revivalist fervor. A long-time Sunday school teacher who knew the Bible well, Emma's religious experience was largely social and cultural, comprised of bake sales and missionary society meetings.

In 1921, when Reverend Hummel, a Baptist evangelist, was invited to hold a two-week revival at the little Methodist church, 14-year-old Kuhlman attended.[48] As she sat in the corner of a pew, she began weeping as the Holy Spirit swept over her for the

47 Buckingham, *Daughter of Destiny*, 19-20.

48 Buckingham, *Daughter of Destiny*, 21.

first time in her life. Not knowing how to respond, she made her way up to a front pew and sat alone, sobbing. Martha Johannssen, a disabled lady from the congregation, handed her a handkerchief and crooned, "'There, there, Kathryn, you've been such a good girl.' 'We both knew she was lying,'" said Kuhlman.[49]

To Kuhlman, her conversion experience was immediately transformational. "Walking back home with Mama, I felt the whole world had changed. I was aware of the flowers that grew along the street. I had never noticed them before. Mr. Kroenoke had gotten a new paint job on his house. But the house hadn't changed. Kathryn Kuhlman had changed. It was the same paint, the same street, the same town. But I was not the same. I was different."[50]

Having completed the tenth grade, Myrtle Parrott extended an invitation to her sister to join the itinerant couple for the summer, and the future evangelist accepted—a pivotal decision that would set the course for the rest of her life.

ITINERATING WITH EVERETT AND MYRTLE PARROTT

Kuhlman's sister's marriage was a turbulent one. Myrtle Parrott had accepted the traveling evangelist's marriage proposal as an opportunity to move out from under her mother's harsh discipline and the monotony of small-town life. Myrtle preached occasionally, but primarily acted as her husband's business

49 Kathryn Kuhlman, "The Beginning of Miracles," Kathryn Kuhlman Foundation, n.d., audiocassette.

50 Buckingham, *Daughter of Destiny*, 22.

manager. Eventually the marriage would end in divorce, but not before Kuhlman joined them at the age of 16 years old.

Kuhlman's beleaguered and weary sister traveled with her husband and their young charge from town to town—the Sawdust Trail—throughout Oregon. The young women sang to the crowds, and eventually Kuhlman was given the opportunity to share her testimony. The people loved her dramatic gestures, which caused Parrott to promise her an opportunity to preach when the time was right. Kuhlman studied hard in between services, spending all of her free time preparing sermons should the promise come to fruition.[51] Her summer stay with the Parrotts became a permanent arrangement, and eventually Parrott would enlist the services of a well-educated and extraordinarily accomplished pianist named Helen Gilliford.[52] Gilliford and Kuhlman became tightly bonded friends, Gilliford taking Myrtle's role of elder sister and mentor.

Parrott's evangelism ministry developed a degree of notoriety. An article announcing the opening of one of Parrott's revival campaigns boasted that he was a "nationally known evangelist" who was associated with the Rev. and Mrs. Howard W. Rusthoi, known as the 'revival broadcasters.' The Rusthois were broadcasting a daily program over KGGC at 4 p.m. They had been heard over twenty-five radio stations from coast to coast and in Mexico.[53] The bright young and eager future evangelist was positioned where first-rate revivalist mentoring would take place.

---

51 Buckingham, *Daughter of Destiny*, 32.

52 Buckingham, *Daughter of Destiny*, 34-35.

53 "Rev. Parrott Will Open Revival Campaign Here," newspaper unknown and n.d., Flower Pentecostal Heritage Center Collection.

BREAKING OUT

As the Parrotts' marriage began to disintegrate into fighting matches, the tent revivals endured the impact. In Boise, Idaho, Parrott did not show up for the scheduled meetings, leaving the women to fend for themselves with very little money. Living on bread and canned tuna, both Gilliford and Kuhlman sank into deep disillusionment. When a Nazarene pastor asked the three women to stay on and continue holding revival services at the Women's Club where they had been ministering, Myrtle, who was packed and ready to join her husband, declined the invitation. She had preached while Gilliford and Kathryn had played and sang. Myrtle protested that they had run out of money. The insistent pastor turned towards Kuhlman and Gilliford, "Well, let the girls stay then."[54]

Kuhlman had wanted to preach, and now she had found her opportunity. Gilliford and Kuhlman would become a ministry team as well as life-long friends. She mused about her first time at the pulpit in those early days during one of her recorded radio talks. She had preached about Zacchaeus in the tree, and then laughed, "But if anyone was up a tree it was me."[55] The young women billed themselves as "God's Girls" and preached throughout the Northwest and Midwest. In Joliet, Illinois, the women were booked for three months of services with the Evangelical Church Alliance. There, Kuhlman was persuaded

54 Buckingham, *Daughter of Destiny*, 35-36.

55 Kathryn Kuhlman, "The Beginning of Miracles," Kathryn Kuhlman Foundation, K832, n.d. radio talk, audio recording.

that she needed to be ordained, and she agreed to it. It was the only ecclesiastical authorization she ever sought or acquired.[56]

SPEAKING IN TONGUES

It was during this series of meetings that the young Methodist evangelist first encountered the Pentecostal experience of glossolalia after praying at the altar for a young woman whom she recalled began to sing beautifully in a heavenly prayer language. The young woman's mother told Kuhlman that previous to the event the girl had been unable to sing a note.[57]

Years later, her services became noted for their ecumenism—with Roman Catholic priests and nuns sitting side by side next to the working poor and young Jesus people hippies—and she did not emphasize the experience but preferred to focus the attention of the crowds on Jesus and not the gift of tongues. However, in the days of Charismatic Revival, when the baptism of the Holy Spirit was a main topic of many sermons, the omission seemed suspect. Critics wondered if she was genuinely Pentecostal. Yet, she clearly represents that she personally experienced the baptism of the Holy Spirit. She said, "I too received the baptism of the Holy Spirit many years ago, but there's never a time when I'm in a great miracle service but what I receive a fresh Baptism of the Holy Spirit."[58]

Kuhlman shared that before she died, Emma Kuhlman had the experience. "Mama never knew there was such a thing; she'd never heard it; she had no light on it; and she wasn't seeking for

---

56 Buckingham, *Daughter of Destiny*, 39.

57 Buckingham, *Daughter of Destiny*, 40.

58 Helen Kooiman Hosier, *Kathryn Kuhlman: A Biography*, (London: Lakeland Books, 1977) 79.

it. I have to believe in an unknown tongue; I have no choice. When Mama opened her eyes, she took my hands in hers, and it was the first time that she had ever approved of me being in this work. She said, 'Kathryn, preach that others may have what I have received.' Mama was never the same.'"[59]

THE GIRL EVANGELIST

Sixteen when she launched out into ministry, Kuhlman was just 21-years-old when thrust into a solo role of evangelist in the summer of 1928. Later in 1937, she would reflect on this season to a reporter for the *Detroit News Pictorial*: "The girl evangelist has no easy time—I work as high as 18 hours a day. She must live in an atmosphere of very watchful care, for there are so many eager to misjudge. She must always be smiling, happy, eager—the feminine relief of tears is denied her…The life is no bed of roses, but I am happy in my work, for I believe in it."[60]

Kathryn lived on nickel rolls, traveled on buses and eventually in an old jalopy,[61] from small town to small town in the Northwest, from Oregon's eastern border to Montana, Idaho, and Wyoming. Years later she recalled, "It seemed I was hungry all the time."[62] She and Gilliford slept in turkey houses or the spare bedroom of a deacon. Joking about the menacing stares from stern photos of

59 Helen Kooiman Hosier, *Kathryn Kuhlman: A Biography,* (London: Lakeland Books, 1977) 136.

60 Wayne E. Warner, *Kathryn Kuhlman: The Woman Behind the Miracles* (Ann Abor, MI: Servant, 1993), 49.

61 Kuhlman quipped that if noise equaled power, referring to the moving of the Holy Spirit in some Pentecostal congregations, then her old car would have been the most powerful vehicle on the road. Kathryn Kuhlman, "An Hour with Kathryn Kuhlman, " n.d., audiocassette.

62 Kathryn Kuhlman, "An Hour with Kathryn Kuhlman, " n.d., audiocassette.

ancestors on their walls, Kuhlman laughed about hiding under quilts from their gaze and for warmth while reading the Bible for countless hours. Bundled under quilts, hiding from the stern eyes of a deacon's grandmother or grandfather, she claimed that she developed her theology by sitting at the feet of the Holy Spirit. "I got my schooling at the feet of the greatest teacher in the world."[63]

Although desperately poor, spending most of her meager funds on posters, handbills, and travel, Kuhlman never doubted her calling. "My call to ministry was just as definite as my conversion." Detractors might challenge her calling to the pulpit, but nothing would stop her. She said that even if everyone in the world told her she was not called "it would have no effect on me whatsoever."[64]

Myrtle recalled that there was a definite time when Kathryn was "called to preach." It came soon after she joined the Parrotts in Oregon. The group had visited a meeting by Dr. Charles Price, and following the meeting Kuhlman began to weep, deeply broken at the prospect of the many who did not accept salvation.

"Didn't you feel it too?" she questioned her sister.

"Feel what?"

"Feel that burden for the lost. I must preach, Myrtle. I'll never be satisfied until I am doing my share."[65]

She responded to that sense of calling with courage and tenacity, even preaching for weeks while standing on a broken ankle. "I used to wait until the famers were through with their milking, their plowing, their harvesting, and when it got dark, they would file in one by one. I've been in every one of those little

63 Buckingham, *Daughter of Destiny*, 48.

64 Warner, *The Woman Behind the Miracles*, 50. See also, Kathryn Kuhlman with Buckingham, *A Glimpse Into Glory*, (Newberry, FL, 1983) 11.

65 Buckingham, *Daughter of Destiny*, 46.

crossroads towns—every one. If the town didn't have a preacher, I offered my services. Nobody really wanted me—I didn't blame them much—but I did say to them, 'Your church is closed anyway. You haven't anything to lose, and you might gain something.'"[66]

GOD'S GIRLS TAKE OFF

The work paid off, and by 1933 God's Girls were loved and respected throughout the Northwest, filling venues with seekers wherever they went. Gilliford was an important ministry partner and friend in these formative years. She was better known in evangelistic circles, having played piano for prominent evangelists of the day, including Uldine Utley, Charles Price, and Watson Argue. Once the pianist for the largest Pentecostal church in the Northwest, Lighthouse Temple, in Eugene, Oregon, with a sixty-piece orchestra and seating for 3,000, Gilliford's training was far more advanced than Kuhlman's. She had attended the University of Oregon for music and the Bible Institute of Los Angeles for the Bible.[67]

The momentum of their ministry reached a crescendo in Idaho at a Twin Falls Methodist Church in January 1933, where they ministered to a crowd of two thousand. Hundreds were turned away in a foreshadowing of things to come. During two and a half weeks of services, 218 people responded to Kuhlman's altar calls and more than 30 people joined the Methodist church.[68]

Humble beginnings provided Kuhlman with a perspective she never lost. "Everybody wants to be a big preacher, a great

66 Kathryn Kuhlman, "The Beginning of Miracles," (K832), audiocassette. See also, Warner, 57.

67 Warner, *The Woman Behind the Miracles*, 51.

68 Warner, *The Woman Behind the Miracles*, 57.

preacher, a famous preacher, a wealthy man, a celebrity...I know where I began. I know from whence I have come."[69]

Following five years on the road, building momentum and experience, God's Girls ventured into Colorado in 1933. Filled with expectancy, the women hired Earl Hewitt, an acquaintance of Gilliford and former manager for Uldine Utley. At the time Hewitt was a credentialed minister with the Assemblies of God.*

THE DENVER REVIVAL TABERNACLE

When they ventured out as a team, Kuhlman and Gilliford initially traveled south from Idaho through Utah, and eventually to Pueblo, Colorado, where they rented an old Montgomery Ward building on Main Street. They remained there for six months.[70] From Pueblo, with her good friend, mentor, and ministry partner beside her, and now a with business manager in addition to a swell of momentum, the team left the dirt roads, dying towns, and closed churches. Did they go to Denver as the result of a strategically planned initiative? One might assume that their new business manager understood the "Girls'" momentum and possibilities and saw the timing was right to advance to a new level. With $5 in their ministry account, they arrived at the mountain city. Ignoring their lack of funds, Kuhlman told Hewitt to go to Denver and rent the largest building he could find, to fill it with chairs, get the finest piano available for Gilliford, and take

69 Kathryn Kuhlman with Jamie Buckingham, *A Glimpse Into Glory*, (Newberry, FL, 1983) 13.

* Hewitt withdrew from the Assemblies of God in 1941.

70 Buckingham, *Daughter of Destiny*, 49.

out a big ad in the *Denver Post* together with spot announcements on all of the radio stations.[71]

The building Hewitt found for God's Girls was almost a duplicate of the building they had used in Pueblo, a Montgomery Ward warehouse located at 1733–37 Champa Street[72] in downtown Denver.[73] Hewitt rented 500 chairs and a grand piano, promising to pay the fee in two weeks. On the first night of her campaign in August 27, 1933, 125 people attended. The following evening boasted more than 400.[74]

For five months the nightly services drew overflow crowds, with Kuhlman and Gilliford staying late at the altar to pray with those who remained for special ministry. When Kuhlman announced that she was ready to move on, a man stood up from the congregation and protested, offering to finance the down payment on the biggest building she could find. It was at this point the vision for the Denver Revival Tabernacle was born.[75] Nevertheless, the team needed to leave the Montgomery Ward warehouse, requiring a temporary move to the Monitor Paper Company at 1941 Curtis Street, which they named the Kuhlman Revival Tabernacle. Gulliford formed a large, one-hundred voice choir, and other evangelists and preachers were invited to fill

71 Buckingham, *Daughter of Destiny*, 57.

72 Jamie Buckingham, *Daughter of Destiny*, 57.

73 Although some discrepancy exists regarding these early venues, early publications report that the Kuhlman meetings were held first at the Montgomery Ward Warehouse, in 1934, then the Kuhlman Revival Temple, the site of the Old Monitor Paper Company in 1934, and finally at the Denver Revival Tabernacle, in an abandoned truck garage, in 1935.

74 Buckingham, *Daughter of Destiny*, 58-59.

75 Buckingham, *Daughter of Destiny*, 60.

out the nightly sermon roster. Kuhlman also launched a radio talk show called *Smiling Through.* Favorite speakers included evangelist Phil Kerr, who introduced Kuhlman to divine healing and instituted a custom of praying for the sick following meetings by anointing them with oil.

In Denver, God's Girls decided to take up residence and launch the Denver Revival Tabernacle at the site of the old warehouse. For five years, the center realized impressive growth. Meetings were held every night except on Monday, and when Kuhlman and Gulliford were away on frequent revival tours, well-known ministers were invited to speak.[76] The Denver Tabernacle became one of the largest revival centers in the region.[77]

THE DEATH OF JOSEPH KUHLMAN

At the pinnacle of her early success, Kuhlman's world was shaken when her beloved father, Joseph A. Kuhlman, 68, was struck by a snow-blinded driver and killed when crossing a street. The Missouri State Board of Health Bureau of Vital Statistics reports that he died on December 30, 1934. The cause of his accidental death was due to a fractured skull.[78] Joseph Kuhlman had been the center of his daughter's life, as the elder, more passive parent to an active child. She often expressed a level of deep devotion throughout her life towards her father. Kuhlman was deeply broken over the loss of her father, and the emotional void may

76 Warner, 60.

77 Warner, 61.

78 Death Certificate Missouri State Board of Health, filed Jan. 2, 1934, by Ferdinand Shryman, and a Supplemental Death Certificate Missouri State Board of Health, dated Jan. 2, 1935.

have influenced a consequential series of destructive decisions that the otherwise judicious, young evangelist made.

In early 1935, just months following the loss of her father, Kuhlman's ministry team located a permanent ministry building. It was an old truck garage, formerly a livery stable, for the Daniele and Fisher Department Store, located at the corner of West Ninth and Acoma Streets.[79] Renovations to the building were finalized on May 30, complete with 2000 seats inside and overshadowed by a grand sign announcing that "Prayer Changes Things." The dedication service that day was held to a standing-room-only crowd. At the close of each service, from 10 to 10:15 p.m., Kuhlman went on the air live over KVOD radio for her program, *Smiling Through.*[80]

It might be said that Kuhlman had two ministries: this first ministry at the end of the Sawdust Trail was part of an evangelism and healing revival that had swept over the American landscape. A second ministry would emerge later. Why two ministries? Sadly, the first one was to end in disaster, as we will see in the next chapter.

79 Buckingham, *Daughter of Destiny*, 67-68.

80 Buckingham, *Daughter of Destiny*, 68.

CHAPTER THREE

God's Girl Takes a Fall

She called herself a "girl evangelist." Together with her musician partner, Helen Gilliford, they traveled during the Great Depression throughout the farmlands of Idaho and Oregon as "God's Girls." With shear tenacity and courage, Kuhlman had plowed through every obstacle, and there were many set up against a young woman in an itinerant ministry. As a traveling "girl evangelist," country churches had sometimes provided sleeping accommodation in a nearby chicken house, where eggs were hatched, or in the freezing attic bedroom of an elderly spinster. She had often gone hungry, surviving on rolls she could purchase for a nickel each. Despite the many hardships, God's Girls had soldiered on to seemingly make it through the toughest times. Just when success smiled her way in Denver, just when her notoriety was rising, crowds were regular, and offerings paid the bills she faced the greatest hurdle of her life. She had met every obstacle and won, and the hardships seemed to be past. But nothing could have prepared her for the greatest challenge of all.

Services at the Denver Tabernacle were off to an impressive start. The radio show *Smiling Through* helped to fill the auditorium regularly. In the style of her unattributed early mentor, Aimee Semple McPherson, Kuhlman would make a grand entrance at every service by appearing at the back of the auditorium and walking down a side aisle where she would wave to her audience and shake their hands. In the style of other female evangelists and pastors of the day, she wore a white "pulpit dress." McPherson and her female ministry students and staff had donned white dresses with capes, possibly mimicking the uniforms of the Salvationists. Even earlier in the century evangelist Maria Woodworth-Etter was known for her white linen dresses. In a religious world in which males were sometimes identified by religious robes and vestments, it might seem that women were choosing their own tradition of religious garb. In a century when hemlines were rising, a modest woman in the pulpit might stand on a raised platform, and, for the sake of modesty, choose a long dress so as not to draw attention to her legs, calves, or ankles, all parts of the body that might be sexualized in the less sanctified minds of a mixed audience.

The Denver Revival Tabernacle was a bustling place, and Kuhlman invited a slate of other speakers. One of the itinerant evangelists invited to speak was Burroughs A. Waltrip. Waltrip was a handsome, young evangelist from Louisiana, with striking black hair, dark, piercing eyes, and a "devastating smile."[81] For an attractive, young, single woman the flashy preacher was a catch.

---

81 Deb Nicklay, "Salvation and Scandal," *The Globe Gazette North Iowa Media Group*, Sunday, January 28, 2007, 1.

Kuhlman fell head-over-heels for him, despite the warnings of friends and guests.

Years later, Kuhlman shared the experience with good friend Viola Malachuk who admitted that "she was really smitten."[82]

Throughout the rest of her life, Kuhlman kept her young marriage to Waltrip a closely guarded secret, and little has been known about him. "Of those Denver years, Kathryn herself was quite silent."[83]

BURROUGHS WALTRIP

He grew up in a Methodist parsonage with a brother who also became a preacher, but Waltrip switched to the Baptist church.[84] Although represented as having only completed one semester of college by biographer Wayne Warner, other records obtained by this author indicate that he attended the Decatur Bible College in Decatur, Texas, where he was pictured in the 1926 *Summit* yearbook as a senior. The yearbook listed his hometown as Wichita Falls,[85] and presents him as an excellent student and class leader. As member of the *Erosphian* literary society, a precursor to present-day fraternities and sororities, Waltrip became a skilled debater, as these societies generally were committed to formal debate.

Waltrip's honors are notable, and include the following: editor of the *Chieftain* for 1925 and 1926, a member of the *Summit*

82 Phone interview with Viola Malachuk, 1/29/11.

83 Helen Kooiman Hosier, *Kathryn Kuhlman, A Biography,* (London: Lakeland Books, 1977), 56–57.

84 Warner, 82.

85 Decatur Bible College, Summit Yearbook, 1926, 27.

staff in 1926, a member of the Pep Squad in 1926, president of B.S.U. in 1925,[86] president of the senior class in 1926, Ero Debater in 1925-26, and an Intercollegiate Debater in 1926. The yearbook applauds him saying that "His active talents accomplished much for D.B.C. (Decatur Bible College)."[87] In 1946, one of the last public records of his ministry involved the establishment of a prayer and fasting center in San Diego, CA, under the leadership of revivalist Franklin Hall. Here, he is referred to as "Dr. Waltrip (Kathryn Kuhlman's husband)."[88] Considering his early academic achievements, he might well have gone on to earn a doctoral degree in later years, although no actual records of advanced degrees have been located.

Growing up, Burroughs Waltrip was the oldest of three children born to Reuben Waltrip, a preacher, and his wife, Lila, in Freestone County, East Texas, according to 1910 Federal Census Records.[89] Reuben Waltrip founded a large Methodist Church in South Austin, TX, which until it was recently demolished bore his name on the cornerstone.[90] In 1918, at age 15, Burroughs lost both his father and younger sister in the 1918 influenza pandemic,

86 Possibly "Baptist Student Union."

87 Decatur Bible College, Summit Yearbook, 1926, 27.

88 Franklin Hall, "Miracle Word" Phoenix; Hall Deliverance Foundation, Inc., Summer 1985. 10; websource: "An Examination of Kingdom, Dominion, and Latter Rain Theology," *Apologetics Index*, http:www.apologeticsindex.org/106.html accessed 1/14/2011.

89 Deb Nicklay, "Salvation and Scandal," *The Globe Gazette North Iowa Media Group*, posted Sunday, January 28, 2007.

90 Email correspondence with Burroughs Waltrip Jr., forwarded personal recollections initially sent to Deb Nicklay of *The Globe Gazette*, sent 1/14/11.

according to Texas death records.[91] Waltrip married Jessie Anna Belle Johnson on December 12, 1926,[92] who bore him two sons, Waltrip Jr. and William.

During his traveling ministry, Waltrip billed himself as "The Louisiana Pulpiteer" and "The Fiery Southerner." Waltrip the son wrote in his recollections, housed at the Mason City Public Library, that this father was a Baptist pastor of two churches before he later discarded his Baptist credentials to become a Pentecostal evangelist.[93] Waltrip Jr. said that his father established his first chapel in Lake Charles, LA, in 1934, at the Calcasieu Tabernacle, using the same method he would use later in Mason City to build the city's Radio Chapel on Pennsylvania Avenue.[94] That method included taking up several offerings during meetings with unabashed appeals for funds.

Waltrip Jr. saw his father as a "dreamer of grandiose dreams, always looking for an opportunity to make a name for himself. He was ever the publicity seeker, advertising as heavily as finances permitted wherever he preached."[95] According to his son, Waltrip wrote flattering newspaper articles about himself in the third person and found startling names for his advertised sermons,

---

91 Deb Nicklay.

92 Ancestry query board response posted by Burroughs Waltrip III, grandson of Burroughs Waltrip, posted March 24, 2004, websource: http://boards.ancestry.com/surnames.waltrip/67.5/mb.ashx, accessed 10/23/10.

93 Deb Nicklay.

94 Deb Nicklay.

95 Personal letter to Geraldine Schwarz from Lt. B.A. Waltrip USN (Ret.), dated 28 June 2004, donated to the collections at the Flower Pentecostal Heritage Center.

such as "The Biggest Sinner in Whatevertownthisis."[96] "And as my mother once commented to me after I reached adulthood, 'he would do anything for money.'"[97] "He loved money!"[98] For example, she told her son that once while she was at work at a secretarial job he sold all of her personal books without her knowledge or permission.

According to his son, Waltrip traveled from his Calcaseiu Tabernacle pastorate to Denver twice taking Waltrip Jr.'s younger brother, Bill, along with him. In late 1935, he left Louisiana and returned exclusively to evangelistic work.[99] Waltrip Jr. recalls that he went one more time to Denver before leaving the family with the maternal grandmother in Austin, TX. Waltrip Jr. also received a letter postmarked from Madison, WI, during the same evangelistic campaign.[100]

In the summer of 1935, just months following the death of Joe Kuhlman, Dennis Brown, a recent convert at the newly erected Denver Tabernacle, claims to have walked past the church office and witnessed Kuhlman and Waltrip locked in an embrace.[101] No confirmation of this matter was every found. Perhaps it took place precisely as described, but it is also possible that the individual saw less than he remembered.

Nevertheless, moving well beyond the point in her young life that a woman might have expected to marry, Kuhlman doubtless

---

96 Personal letter to Geraldine Schwarz from Lt. B.A. Waltrip.

97 Personal letter to Geraldine Schwarz from Lt. B.A. Waltrip USN (Ret.).

98 Burroughs A. Waltrip Jr. personal memoires, written to a journalist to correct an unnamed article, dated 7/22/2002.

99 Burroughs A. Waltrip Jr. personal memoires.

100 Burroughs A. Waltrip Jr. personal memoires.

101 Wayne E. Warner, *Kathryn Kuhlman, the Woman Behind the Miracles*, (Ann Arbor, MI: Servant Publications, 1993), 81.

may have feared the common social stigma of spinsterhood. She spoke of her desire to marry later, saying she would have liked nothing better than to have become one of the Concordia farm wives who collected eggs in the morning, raised a house full of children, and had a man to boss her around.[102] But the story of her relationship with the Texas evangelist and their subsequent marriage and later divorce is not one that Kuhlman shared easily with others. In fact, she spent years recovering from the devastation the misstep caused to her ministry and personal life. What is most surprising is that her ministry recovered at all.

WAS WALTRIP MARRIED?

By all accounts, Waltrip was married when he first met Kuhlman, but what he reported to her regarding his marital status is less certain. Burroughs A. Waltrip, Jr. (the son) insists that the first time his father visited Denver and ministered with Kuhlman was as early as 1934. Kuhlman and Gulliford first arrived in 1933, which suggests the meeting was much earlier than previously indicated by biographers Buckingham and Warner.

> Burroughs (I can't refer to him as "Dad" because he was never a dad to me) and KK began their romance, I feel certain, during the first revival he conducted at her Denver Tabernacle. It could have begun sooner, if the first trip to Denver from Lake Charles, LA, wasn't his first revival at her Tabernacle. He took my three-and-a-half or four-year-old brother with him on the train from Lake Charles to Denver

102 Kathryn Kuhlman,"An Hour With Kathryn Kuhlman," Kathryn Kuhlman Foundation, radio talk, audiocassette.

> for his second (from Lake Charles, in any case) revival at KK's place in Denver. It didn't occur to me until I was grown that my brother was taken along as his "beard." That also explains his taking my brother with him to Denver when we returned from San Diego in 1936.[103]

Authorized biographer, Helen Kooiman Hosier, writing in 1976, said, "I spent a number of hours with Russell Chandler, Religion in the News Editor of the *Los Angeles Times,* and we discussed among other things Miss Kuhlman's reported marriage and divorce and the silence surrounding it. Writers and reporters with a Christian background have, for the most part, respected Miss Kuhlman's wish for privacy and have not belabored the issue regarding this part of her life."[104] Chandler said, "The little-known facts about her marriage and subsequent divorce dealt a severe blow to her burgeoning Denver Revival Tabernacle. Evangelist Burroughs A. Waltrip, who had been a guest speaker in Miss Kuhlman's pulpit, liked more than her church."[105]

Waltrip divorced his wife, Jessie, on June 29, 1937, recorded in Decree N. 13868, District Court, State of Iowa, Marion County: *B.A. Waltrip vs. Jessie Annabelle Waltrip.* Ms. Waltrip did not contest, was granted full custody of the two sons, and the divorce was granted less than two weeks after it was initially filed, according to Warner.[106] "Citing cruel and inhuman treatment 'such as to endanger the life of the plaintiff,' Waltrip obtained a divorce."[107]

---

103 Burroughs A. Waltrip, Jr., email correspondence dated 1/14/2011.

104 Helen Kooiman Hosier, 57.

105 Kooiman Hosier, 57.

106 Warner, 263.

107 Warner, 86.

In contrast, Waltrip Jr.'s (Waltrip's son) personal recollections move the date of filing nearly seven months earlier:

> On Valentine's Day 1937, a moment seared into my memory, Mom opened a letter, in my presence, stating that [Waltrip] was filing for divorce,[108] instead of the Valentine's card she had expected.[109]

In response to the court document citing "cruel and inhuman treatment" on behalf of Jesse Waltrip, Waltrip Jr. says, "This is a vicious lie. My mother was the gentlest and kindest woman I ever knew, ever helping anyone she could who asked. She was the best, actually, the only living example of a *real, true Christian* I have ever seen in my long lifetime, and I include preachers in that statement. She actually practiced Christianity."[110]

Was there any history of violence in Jesse Waltrip's life, as suggested by the divorce decree? Waltrip Jr. says no.

> She never in her life made a threatening statement nor raised a violent hand against anyone, let alone the man she so loved. I can't imagine what prompted my father to allege such false and ugly claims in order to obtain the divorce, and under oath, too! This nasty behavior pretty thoroughly illustrates the kind of liar and sleazy phony he was, wholly lacking in conscience and decency. But, based upon a comment or

108 This may have been informational or the date may have been delayed. Any number of innocent possibilities might explain the difference in dates.

109 Letter from B.A. Waltrip Jr., requesting a correction be made regarding events discussed in an unidentified article, email correspondence dated 7/22/02.

110 Correspondence with Waltrip Jr., on 2/25/2011.

> two by an uncle and others I overheard through the years, I suspect he created the sorry specimen he was all by himself as he grew up. His ego was monumental and he essentially cared for no person but himself, the most wonderful man he knew.[111]

Waltrip Jr. said that, not only did his father neglect to pay the paltry child support payments, he also contacted Jesse through the years when he needed money. Waltrip Jr. remembers multiple "collect telegrams and collect telephone calls over many years in which he asked my mother for money because he was in a jam of one kind or another. Until I was in my mid- or late-teens, she always sent him something. Unlike him, she was unafraid of work and not totally wrapped-up in herself."[112]

Warner details that sixteen months after the divorce was granted Waltrip married Kuhlman in Mason City, Iowa, on October 18, 1938.[113] Waltrip Jr.'s recollections would place the remarriage at eighteen months, but, although the young Waltrip is adamant about his memories, court records confirm that Warner's calculations are accurate.

Kuhlman's marriage to Waltrip also ended in divorce. "The marriage soon dissolved, however, and in the heat of the scandal, the Denver congregation scattered. Miss Kuhlman, who never remarried, was loath to discuss the matter. Old-timers are quoted as saying she suffered over it and repented."[114]

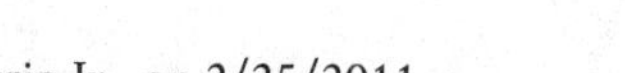

111 Correspondence with Waltrip Jr., on 2/25/2011.

112 Correspondence with Waltrip Jr., on 2/25/2011.

113 Warner, 263.

114 "No Second Miss Kuhlman Apparent," *Los Angles Times*, March 1, 1976, 1, 3.; Helen Kooiman Hosier, *Kathryn Kuhlman, A Biography*, (London: Lakeland Books, 1977), 57.

In the early summer of 1936, Waltrip Sr. went to San Diego, CA, for a revival. Jessie and the children joined him in San Diego that July, driving from Austin to San Diego in a 1934 Chevy that he later sold. Later he traded his own Dodge Coupe in for a brand new 1936 DeSoto. The entire family returned to Austin at the end of the summer in the new car, arriving the day before the children's classes were set to begin.[115] Shortly afterward, Waltrip Sr. left for Denver again, taking the five-year-old Bill with him. The family planned to travel by train to bring Bill back for Christmas. Waltrip Jr., with a case of the measles, stayed home with his grandmother. "So you see, Bill did see him after he had taken up with KK. I believe that he had Bill with him in Denver as a 'cover' for their affair. I never saw him again after the summer of 1936."[116]

INACCURACIES IN THE HISTORICAL RECORD

The personal recollections of Waltrip Jr. challenge Buckingham's record of events. According to Buckingham, Waltrip made his first trip to Denver much later in 1937.[117] Buckingham clearly represents that the Denver congregation was fully aware of the marriage before it took place, and that Kuhlman was aware of the encumbered commitment that Waltrip had made to her. Buckingham wrote: "Everybody in the church in Denver tried to talk Kathryn out of marrying Burroughs Waltrip."[118] In fact,

115 Helen Kooiman Hosier, *Kathryn Kuhlman*, 57.

116 Burroughs A. Waltrip Jr. personal memoires, written to a journalist to correct an unnamed article, dated 7/22/2002.

117 Buckingham, *Daughter of Destiny*, 77.

118 Buckingham, *Daughter of Destiny*, 77.

Buckingham adds that "for a while, back in 1938, it seemed like even God was not big enough to handle His headstrong, redheaded handmaiden. For once in her life she was determined to do things her own way, regardless of what God—or His people—thought about it."[119]

Some readers in that era have noted that when Kuhlman told Buckingham to "tell it all,"[120] she never intended that he include some of the embarrassing details presented in the book.[121] Some of the details included in Buckingham's account of the Kuhlman story have since been challenged by other biographers since it was released as a best-seller in 1976. Nevertheless, Buckingham's account laid the foundation of the popular understanding of the Kuhlman story.

Buckingham reports that Kuhlman invited Waltrip back to the Denver Tabernacle in the fall of 1937. During this second visit, Jessie Waltrip and their two sons came along. "There was some speculation at that time that Jessie was uncomfortable with her rangy, dark haired husband who was spending time with the

---

119 Buckingham, *Daughter of Destiny*, 76.

120 Buckingham, *Daughter of Destiny*, ix.

121 The Kathryn Kuhlman foundation felt the book needlessly dishonored Kuhlman's memory and does not acknowledge it as an official biography. Dino Kartsonakis appeared with Buckingham in 1979 and charged him with sensationalizing Kuhlman's life story on the *PTL* show. He told Buckingham in front of the *PTL* audience that "no woman would have wanted you to say those things written about her. You wrote about her divorce and the flaws of her character and made a big thing about her not wanting to reveal her age. Parts of the book sounded like the *National Enquirer*. You brought things out that no one was talking about and made them conversational again. Kathryn died and your book didn't allow her to go out in glory so that people could remember the wonderful things about her. She never had a chance to defend herself.; Dino Kartsonakis with Cecil Murphey, *Dino, Beyond the Glitz and Glamour, An Autobiography*, (Nashville: Thomas Nelson Publishing, 1990) 158.

long-legged redhead. She wanted to be around to keep an eye on him—and them."[122] Buckingham's description of Kuhlman as a "long-legged redhead" sexualizes the evangelist in a way that seems disrespectful of a woman who devoted herself to a lifetime of service in the kingdom.

Buckingham suggests that "something happened" during Waltrip's second visit to Denver which caused Jessie Waltrip to take the boys and return home to Austin.[123] Then Buckingham adds a benign explanation that "it was time to enter them into school." Here Buckingham seems to be reporting on what *did not happen.* "A month later Waltrip wrote his wife saying he was not coming home. The report that he gave in Denver, however, was that Jessie had deserted him. He had pled, he said, for her to join him, but she refused. Charging her with desertion, he traveled north to the Mason City, Iowa, near the Minnesota border."[124]

DETAILS OF THE NATURE OF THE RELATIONSHIP

Was Kuhlman aware of the fact that Waltrip was still married to Jessie Anna Bell Johnson Waltrip when they first met? Waltrip Jr. equivocates in his assessment of the situation: "I can't imagine that she didn't know he was married and had a family. Of course, he may have told her he had been divorced, etc. I understand he was quite an effective and accomplished con man."[125]

122 Buckingham, *Daughter of Destiny*, 78.
123 Buckingham, *Daughter of Destiny*, 78.
124 Buckingham, *Daughter of Destiny*, 78.
125 Burroughs A. Waltrip, Jr., email correspondence dated 1/15/2011.

Waltrip Jr., who openly expressed his bitterness over his father's betrayal, suspected that Kuhlman knew that Burroughs was married with children when they met. "Inasmuch as he had been with her twice at Denver (from Lake Charles), I can't imagine she didn't know he was married and had a family. Why else would he bring along my little brother when he went to see her? And, of course, the fact he had a small son would tend to tip her off about his wife and family, wouldn't it? She wasn't innocent! She was as phony as he was."[126] As previously noted, Watrip Jr. places his father's first visit to Denver much earlier than Buckingham, as early as 1935. According to Waltrip Jr., the family's visit to Denver was in 1936 not 1937. He confirms that the children were taken back to Austin in order to attend school, but he does not suggest that he was aware of any dramatic event that brought the marriage to an end, as intimated by Buckingham. Waltrip Jr. believes that his mother was first informed of the divorce filing by letter on February 14, 1937, which conflicts with the court documents signed by Jessie Waltrip. Nevertheless, Waltrip Jr. believes that it is possible that Kuhlman was lied to by Waltrip, but remains doubtful, considering her complicit in the entire deception and betrayal of Jessie and the children.

Buckingham writes that at the time of the marriage Waltrip had convinced Kuhlman that Jessie Waltrip had deserted him, which granted him the biblical "right" to freely remarry.[127] "Someone had given Burroughs a book, which he later passed along to Kathryn, putting forth a view that a man and wife were not married in God's sight unless they loved one another when

126 Burroughs A. Waltrip, Jr., email correspondence dated 1/15/2011.
127 Buckingham, *Daughter of Destiny*, 80.

they got married. On the basis of this novel doctrine, Waltrip justified his divorce, claiming that he had never been married in God's sight (even though he had two children) and was free to marry Kathryn. In fact, he advanced the notion that since he had not loved his wife he had been 'living in sin' and was just now repenting and getting his life straightened out."[128]

Regarding the biographical narrative of the historical events surrounding his father, Waltrip Jr. told a reporter, "Jamie Buckingham's 1976 KK-approved biography has many errors of fact concerning Burroughs and is not worth wasting time with."[129] "My mother did not say he was free to marry again because he now said he had never loved her; that is an idiotic concept he developed and proclaimed for himself."[130]

Did the family believe that Kuhlman had been deceived by Waltrip? Waltrip Jr. says that "...his involvement with KK and his desertion of this family are clearly dated.[131] And KK knew from the beginning that he was married and had children. Of course, we have no way of knowing what kind of wild and distorted yarns he spun for her. It may be possible that he claimed Mom had deserted him because she insisted on remaining in Austin so we boys could go to school. He had made her leave me with her mother repeatedly when I was still a baby. And one entire school

128 Buckingham, *Daughter of Destiny*, 80.

129 Letter to Geraldine Schwarz from Lt. B.A. Waltrip, USN (Ret.) dated 28 June 2004, housed in the Flower Pentecostal Heritage Collection.

130 Letter from Waltrip Jr. requesting a correction to an article. Letter is dated July 22, 2002.

131 The dates based upon Waltrip Jr.'s childhood memories might seem to conflict with court records, especially since some are in direct conflict with court records.

semester I lived with her sister and family while they were on the road. I think it is more like he deserted us, long before he filed for divorce."[132]

Jessie Waltrip died on November 8, 1996. She never remarried, and in the concluding year of her life confided to Waltrip Jr.'s wife that she still loved Waltrip.[133]

RADIO CHAPEL

Waltrip is generally remembered by his family as a con artist, manipulator—a smooth talker and spell-binder who in another century might have been considered deeply narcissistic or even sociopathic.[134] He was handsome, brilliant, a winning speaker who went from divorcing his wife and leaving his children to

---

132 Letter from Waltrip Jr. requesting a correction to an article. Letter is dated July 22, 2002.

133 Waltrip Jr. letter to Deb Nicklay, journalist for *The Globe Gazette North Iowa Media Group*, n.d., forwarded to Peggy de Alminana from Deb Nicklay January 24, 2011.

134 Antisocial personality disorder (APD) is a personality disorder which is often characterized by antisocial and impulsive behavior. APD is generally considered to be the same as, or similar to, the disorder that was previously known as psychopathic or sociopathic personality disorder. Approximately 3% of men and 1% of women have some form of antisocial personality disorder (source: DSM-IV). Although criminal activity is not a necessary requirement for the diagnosis, these individuals often encounter legal difficulties due to their disregard for societal standards and the rights of others. Therefore, many of these individuals can be found in prisons. However, it should be noted that criminal activity does not automatically warrant a diagnosis of APD, nor does a diagnosis of APD imply that a person is a criminal. It is hypothesized that many high achievers exhibit APD characteristics. Research has shown that individuals with APD are indifferent to the possibility of physical pain or many punishments, and show no indications that they experience fear when so threatened; this may explain their apparent disregard for the consequences of their actions, and their lack of empathy when others are suffering.

building one of the most unique and modern ministry facilities in Iowa. Iowans remember him in caricature, as another Harold Hill of *The Music Man* who came into a small town in Iowa for the purpose of bilking naïve townsfolk out of their hard-earned money.

> In that Depression Era people in this town, and probably others, were looking for someone who would inspire them and lead them out of the doldrums. The fact that in less than a year a preacher could form a congregation and move from a tent to an amazing structure that is still dynamic is remarkable. And although that story is true, it may have been a springboard for another story. I think it is not by accident that Meredith Wilson wrote *The Music Man* about a super-salesman who came to Mason City and stirred the towns-people to frenzy over a boy's band! And Mason City is still known for its school music programs and marching bands.[135]

Waltrip is remembered by Iowans for fleecing the flock to gain funds, running up debts that he did not repay, and building a monument to himself, and a ministry based on deceit that finally caught up with him. Waltrip came to Mason City, IA, in 1937, and, despite the poverty of the Depression Era, he collected impressive sums of money to build the Radio Chapel, which today is home to KIMT-TV studios on Pennsylvania Ave. Named

135 Letter from Gerry Schwarz to Burroughs Waltrip, Jr. dated July 6, 2004, archived in the Flower Pentecostal Heritage Center Collections, The Assemblies of God Headquarters, Springfield, MO. Schwarz was an English instructor at North Iowa Area Community College, who wrote articles about Waltrip and the Radio Chapel.

"Radio Chapel" in a time when owning a home radio seemed totally new and modern, this facility was completely unique to its time in many other ways, especially in Iowa. "The 96-foot-by-64-foot main hall had no outside windows, recessed lighting, a choir area accented with stars, and a pulpit that rose up through the floor. No hymnals were necessary, since a 'stereopticon'[136] device flashed words on a screen. Clouds seemingly floated across the ceiling."[137] The chapel was built to look "as smart as tomorrow's sunrise" Waltrip told the local paper.[138]

When funds for the chapel did not come in as quickly as Waltrip anticipated, he told the congregation that he intended to fast until they did. Local historian Gerry Schwarz revealed that in her compilation of local historical research she spoke with a cab driver who picked him up. Townsfolk recall that he used a wheelchair as a prop to elicit sympathy during the fund-raising campaign:

> He was staying at the Hanford Hotel and taking a taxi to the tent meetings which were held at the future site of the Radio Chapel. Clete Heidenreich was the taxi driver assigned to pick him up and deliver him to the meeting. When Clete would drive to the hotel, Waltrip would come out pushing his wheelchair. He would put it in the taxi, climb in, and ride to the tent. Then Clete was told to take the wheelchair

---

136 Hymnals would continue to be a staple in worship services until well into the 1960s and 1970s, making this precursor to current Chyrons far advanced for its time.

137 Deb Nicklay, "Salvation and Scandal," *The Globe Gazette North Iowa Media Group*, posted Sunday, January 28, 2007, 4.

138 Deb Nicklay, "Salvation and Scandal," 4.

> out, help the weak and starving man out of the taxi, set him in the wheelchair and push him up to the front. As Clete returned to the taxi, he found a candy wrapper on the seat. So much for fasting.[139]

The formal dedication of the chapel took place in 1938. However, almost immediately after Waltrip's marriage to Kuhlman in October of the same year, rumors of his divorce began to surface. Soon a series of lawsuits followed.

ANOTHER 'OTHER' WOMAN?

Schwarz recounted another story about the event. It seems that when Waltrip attempted to purchase a large life insurance policy, the agent told him that a cuckholded husband had threatened to kill Waltrip should he find him. Jim Otzen, the insurance man, told Schwarz that when he visited the insurance headquarters over the matter he was told, "Well you see, Mr. Otzen, your Mr. Waltrip stole some other guy's wife down in Florida and ran off with her."[140]

Local researchers have assumed that the other woman described by the insurance man was Kuhlman, but she did not fit the description in that she was unmarried and not from Florida. In additional references, the other woman in Waltrip's life was referred to as a "blonde bombshell," but Kuhlman had

139 Letter from Gerry Schwarz to Burroughs Waltrip, Jr. dated July 6, 2004, achieved in the Flower Pentecostal Heritage Center Collections, The Assemblies of God Headquarters, Springfield, MO. Schwarz was an English instructor at North Iowa Area Community College, who wrote articles about Waltrip and the Radio Chapel.

140 Letter from Gerry Schwarz to Burroughs Waltrip, Jr. dated July 6, 2004.

red and not blonde hair. One might surmise that Waltrip's philandering stretched beyond his relationship with Kuhlman.[141] The possibility of another 'other' woman might actually solve some of the timeline and other factual difficulties and conflicts noted earlier. Perhaps at least some of the story's details attributed to Kuhlman might actually pertain to the "Blonde Bombshell" other woman in Waltrip's life.

DISGRACED AND REJECTED

According to the *Mason City Globe Gazette,* in May 1939, Waltrip and Kuhlman, $40,000.00 in debt, and after a sheriff's auction had been planned and withdrawn, announced that the church had failed. Waltrip told his congregation that "only a miracle in a day or two could save the doors from closing." He warned businesses that might intend to purchase the structure that "no business will ever prosper here," adding there was a "curse" on the city. "The people of this town have turned down the house of God and I feel sorry for Mason City because of it." He asked the audience for a

141 At 3:37 pm on 1/28/2011 Gerry Schwarz responded to my email inquiry. She wrote: Dear Peggy, What fun it was to see the name of Burroughs Waltrip on my inbox. Most of the stories I wrote about him came from people who had known him back in the '30s and '40s. Our friend who sold life insurance was not able to write a policy for Waltrip because he was a poor risk—the husband of Waltrip's girlfriend had promised to kill him! Waltrip posed as a single man while he was in Mason City, so the fact that he and Kathryn Kuhlman were "keeping company" did not raise too many eyebrows, but if they had known he had a wife and two sons in Texas...well, we can only imagine! ... His son hinted that there were more girlfriends before and after Kathryn. Apparently she did not look into his past or present before they eloped. I know you are having a good time researching this topic. Thanks for writing. Gerry Schwarz.

$100 offering to pay his personal bills and start over in another town, but only $35 was collected. A few days later, Kuhlman and Waltrip left town together.[142]

On her part in this dramatic ministry calamity, Kuhlman had been completely taken in by him, and, following the same pattern set by his first wife, loved him deeply until she died. Kuhlman shared her feelings for Waltrip with her friend Viola Malachuk. "He told her, 'If you go you will never see me again,' and she never did."[143] She received a valentine every year from an anonymous sender she believed came from Waltrip. Kuhlman never remarried and never formed a romantic attachment to any other man.

It seems palpable that, just as Waltrip had skillfully manipulated to his own ends an entire city in Iowa, he was certainly capable of successfully doing the same with the tender, young Kuhlman's affections. Her success at the Denver Tabernacle would be seen, from the perspective of a charlatan and con artist, as a prize plum easy to be picked. What is revealing about Kuhlman is not that she was taken in by a skilled con artist who presented himself as the abandoned spouse of Jessie Annabelle Waltrip, using skillful manipulation that his son does not deny. What reveals her character is the fact that, having come to the full realization of the matter, she was then willing to walk away and remain unmarried. She might have argued before a court that having been deceived before entering into the contract of marriage she therefore had the right of annulment, but she did

142 Deb Nicklay, 6-7.

143 Phone interview with Viola Malachuk, 1/29/11.

not.[144] Although she left Waltrip in 1944, he did not divorce her until 1948 when a sheriff quietly served her the papers in Franklin, PA, where she had eventually reemerged as a full-time minister.[145]

HITTING THE SAWDUST TRAIL

Kathryn Kuhlman left home to minister as part of the Sawdust Trail tent revival. It was as untamed at the time as were many of the remote country towns and villages where she traveled. Healing evangelists lit the fires of revival throughout the young American nation and spread the message of holiness and Pentecostal fire to farms and cottages throughout the Midwest and South. Waltrip did not stand alone among charlatans and fast-talking swindlers who charmed the naïve and simple country folk they visited. In fact, elements of manipulation seeped into some of the most scrupulously honest of ministries on the Sawdust Trail. The well-trodden path of the evangelism and healing revivalists that Kuhlman had chosen to walk upon was covered with many branches and brambles, twists, turns, rocks and blockages. Her early fall into danger nearly ended her ministry on that rocky path. Perhaps the greatest miracle of all in her young life was that it did not.

---

144 Annulment is a way of terminating a marriage that is different from divorce and separation. Annulment is the process of nullifying of a marriage where the court declares that the marriage never took place. In order to annul a marriage, the person seeking the legal action must have sufficient grounds for annulment. Grounds for annulment typically involve one party's lack of capacity for marriage or some type of fraud.

145 Roberts Liardon, *Kathryn Kuhlman, A Spiritual Biography of God's Miracle Working Power*, (Tulsa, Ok.: Harrison House, 1990), 58.

To gain further insight and context into the time and ministry culture that schooled the young future healing evangelist, and that introduced her to a theological foundation that she eventually rejected, the next chapter we will examine more closely the world of healing and evangelistic revivalism in the early and mid-20th century's heartland.

CHAPTER FOUR

"And a Highway Shall Be There"

"Father, you are able to take these tumors off of this man's spinal cord." A sweating evangelist shouts his prayer: "Let him run like Elijah. Let him run like the prophets of old." A.A. Allen's voice booms over a giant tent of seekers whose roaring, clapping celebration fills a hot, dusty tent.[146] The seeker lies moaning on a stretcher, a private nurse seems to govern the interaction as the wizened man thrashes about and the evangelist lays his hands upon the man's useless limbs. In a burst of energy, the man begins to lift his legs by his own power as the evangelist jumps up and down screaming. Now the frail body jumps up and begins to run. The crowd explodes. Allen was one of a long line of evangelists whose itinerant tent ministries littered the American landscape

146 https://www.youtube.com/watch?v=pZZV_yr5chI accessed 2/20/21.

in the early twentieth century healing revivals. The noisy ritual is incomplete at this point; for a testimony will follow to celebrate the miraculous event.

The ministry of healing has accompanied evangelism since the time of Christ. For many centuries after Christ, however, the healing message lay dormant in most, but not all, religious groups. During the late 19th and early 20th centuries, there were hundreds, probably thousands, of healers and healing evangelists—both well-known and obscure—whose faith and work would pave the pathway for Sawdust Trail revivals. This chapter will look at a few exemplars to provide a context for Kuhlman's work.

The theology of healing evolved through the late 19th and early 20th centuries, but as we will see, it was Kathryn Kuhlman who brought the most dramatic and positive changes to the way American seekers understood the healing power of God.

HEALING IN THE ATONEMENT

Throughout the healing movements in the past, the one constant tenet was the understanding that healing is provided to the believer as part of the atonement. The roots of this understanding came from Charles Wesley and early Methodism. "Wesley was deeply influenced by Puritanism (which rejected current-day healing on the basis of a dispensationalism that taught the miraculous had ended), but also was in tension with it. Moreover, through his parents Wesley was a product of the Anglican high church tradition with its tendency to preserve a doctrine of the miraculous."[147]

147 Donald W. Dayton, *Theological Roots of Pentecostalism,* (Metuchen, NJ: Hendrickson Publishers, Inc., 1987), 117.

Wesley's *Journal* often mentions events that would today count as miraculous healings.[148]

Of particular note is Wesley's "therapeutic" model of grace and salvation.[149] "Grace was the cure for the disease of sin, and the two-fold nature of the Wesleyan view of salvation (justification and sanctification[150]) was often described as the 'double cure.'"[151] Wesley believed strongly in the present power of God to make a believer's life free from the many sins that plague human beings. He wondered if the saved person was able to be fully restored to the image of God, then perhaps even the physical body could be freed from sickness and disease, which Wesley saw as resultant of the Fall of humankind into sin.[152]

---

148 T. Kelsey, *Healing and Christianity in Ancient Thought and Modern Times*, (NYC: Harper and Row, 1976), 235; see also, footnote 44. See also, Donald W. Dayton, *Theological Roots of Pentecostalism*, 118.

149 "Wesley was so concerned about physical health that his best-selling book was a collection of what we would call homeopathic medicine called Primitive Physic [see, Primitive Physic: or An Easy and Natural Method of Curing Most Diseases, (Philadelphia: Parry Hall, 1791)]. His understanding of salvation was broad and inclusive and completely grounded in Christ's atonement. He saw the power of God eventually renewing the whole cosmos, including physical health. So though he did not have what we would call a healing ministry, his holistic view of salvation certainly inspired later holiness Wesleyans who were faith healers, albeit in a less theologically comprehensive way. You might say they dumbed down his view of the effects of cosmic redemption in the practice of faith healing, though they were inspired by his view that salvation cannot be limited to the spiritual alone," Nathan W. Attwood, email correspondence dated 10/24/2020.

150 Justification is the right-standing the believer enters into upon salvation and sanctification is the actual righteousness promised to those who walk closely with the Lord.

151 Donald W. Dayton, *Theological Roots of Pentecostalism*, 119.

152 Donald W. Dayton, *Theological Roots of Pentecostalism*, 119.

In pre-Civil War America, revivalist Charles Finney[153] adopted many of Wesley's views on sanctification. Revivalism swept the nation and coalesced with a burgeoning Methodism, which came to be known as the Holiness Movement due to its emphasis on righteous living. The 1830s rising emphasis on 'Christian perfection' sparked the Holiness Crusade. Phoebe Palmer, considered a firebrand, theologian, and practitioner of Holiness, developed Wesley's message of holiness further by teaching that Christians could indeed receive 'perfection' through a second touch (with salvation being the first touch) of God's grace upon their lives. She took Wesley's hope of holy living in this lifetime to the next level. As a prolific writer and teacher, influenced greatly by Finney, she developed the present-day understanding of the altar call. Palmer's understanding consisted of having child-like faith, a simplicity which, without reasoning, takes God at his word.

---

153 Charles Grandison Finney (August 29, 1792 – August 16, 1875) was an American Presbyterian minister and leader in the Second Great Awakening in the United States. He has been called the "Father of Modern Revivalism." Finney was best known as a flamboyant revivalist preacher from 1825 to 1835 in the Burnedover District in Upstate New York and Manhattan, an opponent of Old School Presbyterian theology, an advocate of Christian perfectionism, and a religious writer.

Together with several other evangelical leaders, his religious views led him to promote social reforms, such as abolitionism and equal education for women and African Americans. From 1835 he taught at Oberlin College of Ohio, which accepted students without regard to race or sex. He served as its second president from 1851 to 1865, and its faculty and students were activists for abolitionism, the Underground Railroad, and universal education. See https://en.wikipedia.org/wiki/Charles_Grandison_Finney.

"ACCEPT IT BY FAITH"

Where Wesley had written of emotion and experience being involved with sanctification, Palmer saw it as gift of God to be claimed by faith. Palmer wrote that Jesus's atoning blood is the only thing that can wash away the stain of sin, and no one needs to wait to feel an emotion to claim it. She invited believers to come to the altar and make a simple request for the gift of holiness. They did not have to wait for Jesus to signal them with a feeling to claim holiness. To receive entire sanctification, one simply had to call on Jesus as Lord and make total surrender to him. One simply had to claim his or her holiness before God, acknowledging it was only available through Jesus and his blood.[154] Many believers making that claim filled the altars with prayer seeking God for a special touch that would in a moment break the power of sin and make them holy, or sanctified. The special grace or gift of holiness or sanctification came to be recognized as a "second blessing" beyond the initial experience of salvation.

> ...all the Lord's ransomed ones, who have been so fully redeemed, and chosen out of the world, should be sanctified, set apart for holy service, as chosen vessels unto God, to bear his hallowed name before a gainsaying world, by having the seal legibly enstamped upon the forehead, proclaiming them as 'not of the world,' a 'peculiar people,' to show forth His praise..."'[155]

154 See Phoebe Palmer, *The Way of Holiness: Notes by the Way*, (Salem, OH: Schmul Publishing Co., Inc., 1988).

155 Phoebe Palmer, *The Way of Holiness*, 33.

The Holiness Movement that followed set the world ablaze as men and women, filled with evangelical fervor, preached the message of sanctification, offering a stale church the possibility of sinless cleansing through living faith in the blood of Jesus Christ. The ground was laid for another wave of healing revivalism: the "Faith-Cure Movement."

FAITH-CURE'S LONG REACH

The Divine Healing Movement flowed directly out of the Holiness Movement. Initially, it was called the "Faith-Cure Movement." "Faith-Cure" was coined by Dr. Charles Cullis of Boston, credited by some for the modern movement, in the early 1870s.[156] A doctor of homeopathic medicine, he began to incorporate the prayer of faith in his practice, based upon James 5:14–15: " Is any sick among you? Let him call for the elders of the church; and let them pray over him, anointing him with oil in the name of the Lord: And the prayer of faith shall save the sick, and the Lord shall raise him up; and if he have committed sins, they shall be forgiven him (KJV)." He claimed that hundreds of suffers were healed based upon his faith in this verse of Scripture.[157]

In time, Cullis was able to convince other Holiness adherents that, just like salvation, healing was provided for in the atonement of Christ.[158]

---

156 Kimberly Ervin Alexander, *Pentecostal Healing: Models in Theology and Practice*, (Dorset, UK: Deo Publishing, 2006) 9.

157 Kimberly Ervin Alexander, *Pentecostal Healing*, 16.

158 Kimberly Ervin Alexander, *Pentecostal Healing*, 17.

Ethan O. Allen, a lay person, was one of the first to link Christian Perfection with divine healing.[159] After experiencing a healing in his own body, he began traveling with an African-American couple, Sarah and Edward Mix, to proclaim the message of healing. He writes:

> For several years my mind had been exercised before God as to whether it was not his will that the Work of Faith in which he had placed me, should extend to the cure of disease, as well as the alleviation of the miseries of the afflicted.[160]

Other notable figures in the early movement who further developed the understanding of healing in the atonement include A.B. Simpson, founder of the Christian Missionary Alliance, and A.J. Gordon, founder of the college with his name.

Healing and Holiness became even more closely connected in the ministry of Episcopalian Carrie Judd Montgomery, who was deeply influenced by Sarah Mix and Cullis.[161]

CARRIE JUDD MONTGOMERY

Montgomery is among the early pioneers who rejected medicine. "Carrie ... told people to throw out all medicine so that they could act in faith and rely on the Great Physician alone for their healing. Carrie believed that clinging onto medicine implied a 'lack of faith.'"[162] Eventually, the wholesale rejection of medicine would become a troublesome tenet of the early teachings on healing.

---

159 Kimberly Ervin Alexander, *Pentecostal Healing,* 15.

160 Donald W. Dayton, *Theological Roots of Pentecostalism,* 123.

161 Donald W. Dayton, *Theological Roots of Pentecostalism,* 125.

162 Jennifer A. Miskov, *Life on Wings: The Forgotten Life and Theology of Carrie Judd Montgomery (1858-1946),* (Cleveland, TN: CPT Press, 2012), 147.

Montgomery taught that in every instance God willed for the sick to be healed, and that any failure to realize healing lay in the weak faith of the seeker. Montgomery also encouraged the sick to deny their physical symptoms. "Carrie taught that people should deny those symptoms and believe what God's word said about their healing whether they experienced the physical improvement or not."[163] What may have begun as an effort to encourage faith in the needy seeker later became a matter of laying blame. In time, the sick could be seen leaving many healing services seemingly beaten down, ruefully criticizing themselves for the lack of faith that hindered God's healing hand.

Montgomery spans both the Holiness and the later Pentecostal movements but remains within the Christian Missionary Alliance camp, which rejected glossolalia (the gift of speaking in tongues) and renounced the doctrine of the baptism of the Holy Spirit. This division between the movements eventually became contentious, and Montgomery's ability to remain in good favor within both sides seems somewhat remarkable.[164]

Human effort and divine agency created a tightrope that many in the early movement were forced to traverse, and detractors long have criticized these early healing movements as tending towards human or self-effort, also known as Pelagianism.[165] William K. Kay wrote eloquently regarding this razor's edge that the sick

---

163 Jennifer A. Miskov, *Life on Wings*, 174.

164 See Jennifer A. Miskov, *Life on Wings: The Forgotten Life and Theology of Carrie Judd Montgomery (1858-1946)* (Cleveland, TN: CPT Press, 2012).

165 Pelagianism received its name from Pelagius and is considered a heresy of the fifth century that denied original sin as well as Christian grace. It taught that salvation was attainable through self-effort and that Christ was merely an example whose works can be followed through human effort without the help of divine agency and grace.

were forced to walk between faith and healing: "To upgrade faith is to risk condemning the unhealed for their own illnesses and, worse, to make them feel guilty that they even asked for prayer. To downplay faith is to risk pushing healing back behind a barrier of divine inscrutability. Healing becomes conditional upon God's mysterious will, and human beings cannot do very much to find what this will is or to make it happen."[166]

ALEXANDER DOWIE

One of the most radical and flamboyant Holiness healers was Alexander Dowie, who built Zion City, IL, a visionary city that celebrated faith and holiness teachings. He dominated the Divine Healing Movement, founded in 1890.[167] Dowie was bold and unapologetic in his defense of the power of God to heal. He condemned all medicines, medical treatments, and medical doctors of being agents of Satan, and demanded that true saints depend upon God alone for healing.[168] In 1895, Dowie was arrested for practicing medicine without a license and spent 120 days answering more than 100 arrest warrants. Although he had once worked for medical profession as surgical assistant in Scotland,[169] he condemned it harshly:

> I want to say today that doctors as a profession are directly inspired by the devil. All doctors are poisoner-general and

---

166 William K. Kay and Anne E. Dyer, *Pentecostal and Charismatic Studies: A Reader*, 2004, 47.

167 Donald W. Dayton, *Theological Roots of Pentecostalism*, 136.

168 Vinson Synan, "A Healer in the House? A Historical Perspective on Healing in the Pentecostal/Charismatic Tradition," *AJPS* 3/2 (2000) 193.

169 See Vinson Synan, "A Healer in the House?" 193.

> surgical butchers and professional destroyers. They are monsters who hold in their hands deadly poisons and deadly surgical knives, and in the name of law demand that you lie down upon the altar of their operating tables, that they may deprive you of your consciousness and make you a living sacrifice.[170]

He founded the Christian Catholic Church where he called believers into a war together with him against established religion. By 1900, he began construction of Zion City, located north of Chicago, with plans to house 200,000 holiness residents. There, profanity, vulgarity, sorcery, and "medical poisoners" were strictly forbidden. There was to be no dancing, alcohol, tobacco, vaccinations, drugs or physicians, and no unclean foods such as oysters and swine.[171] Dowie's strong bias against medical doctors and medicine took hold of the early movement and would become the view of many Holiness and early Pentecostal leaders. He was ahead of his time in other ways.

Dowie foresaw the advent of both the radio and the television long before these modern communication systems were invented. "His prophetic insight was remarkable, and he predicted things which only recently have come to pass. For example, in a meeting held in Chicago, on Sept. 5, 1897, he prophesied of the radio in the following words:

> Am I going to speak to 300,000 people every Sunday afternoon? Why, we are going to do it. Do you not know

170 Alexander Dowie, "Doctors, Drugs and Devils," Or the Foes of Christ the Healer," *Physical Culture* (April, 1895) 81-86.

171 Public access: http://www.forensicgenealogy.info/images/tobacco_sign_2.jpg.

> that one day in the big Zion Temple that we will have, we are going to have a great big thing to catch the sound and I am going to have them TURN ON ZION TO ZION'S FRIENDS IN NEW YORK. See! And by the beds of sick and sorrowing, some day, I am going to have them hear the testimonies that they cannot hear except from dying beds. Going to get it some day. It has to be done. It is going to be done because the mouth of the Lord spoke that a long time ago. Do you know it?[172]

At another time he prophesied of the advent of television, speaking of its possibilities in a sermon preached October 16, 1904.

> I know not the possibilities of electricity. It is possible that it may yet CONVEY THE FACE OF THE SPEAKER, and, by photo-electricity, show the man as he is talking. Perhaps a discourse delivered here may be heard in every city of the United States. SOME DAY THAT WILL BE SO AND THE WORD SPOKEN IN SHILOH TABERNACLE WILL BE HEARD EVEN IN THE FARTHEST CORNERS OF THE EARTH."[173]

Seeming ever more unhinged, Dowie's leadership became increasingly authoritarian until he proclaimed himself "Elijah the Restorer" in 1901. "The declaration was so startling in its nature as to leave his own people, when they heard it, almost breathless with astonishment. For it was nothing less than an avowal that

---

172 Gordon Lindsay, *Alexander Dowie, A Life Story of Trials, Tragedies, and Triumphs* (Dallas, TX: Christ for the Nations, reprint 1980) 133-134. See also, *Leaves of Healing* Vol. 16, No. 1, 15.

173 Gordon Lindsay, *Alexander Dowie, A Life Story of Trials, Tragedies, and Triumphs* (Dallas, TX: Christ for the Nations, reprint 1980) 133-134.

he, John Alexander Dowie, was Elijah, the Restorer, whose return to earth was spoken of many centuries before by the prophets!"[174] Dowie shocked crowds when he entered into meetings donning the tunic and turban of a high priest in his attempt to establish himself in the role of Elijah. He suffered a stroke in 1905, which left him severely disabled, a living vegetable. In 1907, Dowie died in disgrace, rejected and ignored by the followers that once adored him.[175]

Dowie's influence had helped to inspire another wave of healing ministry.

PENTECOSTAL HEALING

By the turn of the 20th century, most nascent Pentecostal currents had adopted the message of healing as an integral part of faith. Early Pentecostalism leader Charles Fox Parham had visited Dowie's healing home and returned to Topeka, KS, to start one of his own.[176] It was there that a student, Agnes Ozman, after a long season of prayer, burst forth in a prayer language she had never learned, and the miracle of speaking in tongues was restored to the church. (See Mark 16:17: "And these signs shall follow them that believe; In my name shall they cast out devils; they shall speak with new tongues, KJV.") Another Parham student, William J. Seymour, an African American man, took the teaching about speaking in tongues to Los Angeles and ignited and led the Azusa Street Revival. Healings and miracles played a

174 Gordon Lindsay, *Alexander Dowie, A Life Story*, 135.

175 Vinson Synan, "A Healer in the House?" 195.

176 Vinson Synan, "A Healer in the House?" 195.

significant role in the new movement that would spread around the world in a matter of just decades.

AIMEE SEMPLE MCPHERSON

As the early 20th Century moved forward, several waves of healing revival swept across the religious landscape that were associated with the Pentecostal Outpouring. Aimee Semple McPherson's life and ministry bridged the events at Azusa Street (she and her husband Robert Semple studied directly under Durham, an important early leader linked to Azusa).

Wildly popular throughout the early 20th century, McPherson held healing rallies that drew crowds of thousands into large auditoriums and open-air venues. This tireless pioneer of Pentecost laid hands on nearly every needy head as hundreds declared they received a healing touch from above.[177] When she used auditoriums, the press of the multitudes of the sick forced her to move out of doors to healing rallies, where she anointed and prayed for every person in vast healing lines. "In 1921, for example, police estimated that fully half the population of San Diego jammed Balboa Park for two days of healing meetings... Whether or not healings occurred was not always the point: the press noted that McPherson brightened the days of the desperately ill and that they seemed to benefit, even if temporarily, from her prayers."[178]

177 Edith L. Blumhofer, "Reflections on the Source of Aimee Semple McPherson's Voice," *Pneuma, the Journal for the Society of Pentecostal Studies*, (Vol. 17, No. 1, Spring 1995), 23; Frances Wayne, "Healer Visits Denver Underworld to Seek Saving of Souls," *The Denver Post*, 2 July 1921, 5.

178 Edith L. Blumhofer, "Reflections on the Source of Aimee Semple McPherson's Voice," 5.

Although she launched her own denomination arising from the organic overgrowth of her Los Angeles work, much of her outreach began and remained committed to a new kind of ecumenism that presaged the Charismatic Renewal, which would come decades later and was linked to Kuhlman's ministry. McPherson's early tent revivals, that later grew to giant auditoriums and outdoor stadiums, were always comprised of seekers from many diverse denominations and backgrounds. McPherson died in 1944 at the age of 53.

ORAL ROBERTS (1918-2009)

The son of a Pentecostal preacher, Oral Roberts became an itinerant evangelist and faith healer in the late 1940s. The Oral Roberts Evangelistic Association, based in Tulsa, OK, served as the parent organization for other endeavors, including a publishing firm and, eventually, television. Starting in the 1950s, Roberts became the second person to launch an evangelistic television show, with Rex Humbard being the first. Roberts was able to reach a wide audience through radio and television. In 1963 he founded Oral Roberts University in Tulsa, where he served as chancellor.[179]

Roberts' early ministry career was part of a tent revival movement that lasted for decades throughout the South and Midwest. These faith healers all claimed the healing power of God visited a sick body based upon the faith of the seeker. Lines of sick and needy attendees fill the tents as the evangelist laid

179 Matt Stefon, Assistant Editor, "Oral Roberts American Evangelist," *Encyclopaedia Britannica*, https://www.britannica.com/biography/Oral-Roberts. Accessed 7/15/2020.

hands on every head, often anointed with oil, and rebuked the sickness or disease. Attendants passed out cards upon which the illness was written, and after a long wait in line, many struggling with weakness and pain, the supplicant would hand the card to the healer and declare his faith to the congregation. Those who left unhealed were admonished to build up their faith.

Allen Spraggett, an unbeliever with a keen interest in the supernatural, visited a Roberts tent meeting in 1963 and wrote about it in a discussion of healing ministries and Kathryn Kuhlman. He said,

> My personal experiences with faith healers, including those I've observed as an investigative reporter, have been considerable and, in many cases, negative.... In August 1963, Rev. Oral Roberts of Tulsa, Oklahoma, the high priest of contemporary big-shot faith healers descended on Toronto like a ball of fire. Ten thousand persons every night packed his 'canvas cathedral,' as Roberts called the huge tent in which he held his meetings. Night after night I watched as the lame, the blind, and the deaf filed past him in the ritual of prayer and the laying on of hands.[180]

Spraggett chronicled his disappointment over the methods and disappointing results he witnessed and was highly critical of all tent revivalists and healing evangelists but Kuhlman. Several common features troubled him:

> The practice of requiring people to sign cards describing their ailments before admitting them to the healing line to

180 Allen Spraggett, *Kathryn Kuhlman, The Woman Who Believed in Miracles,* (New York: The American Library, Inc., 1970), 28.

> be prayed for also bothered me. It could be a ploy to screen the easy cases from the difficult ones, making sure that the evangelist was not confronted by persons who were unlikely to respond to his particular brand of shock therapy.[181]

Spraggett was skeptical of Roberts for other reasons. He strongly objected to segregating the extremely ill and infirm in a separate tent, called the "invalids' tent," which was kept "away from the prying eyes of the public. ... Not one of the invalids I observed showed the slightest improvement after the evangelist's brief visit."[182]

In fairness to Roberts, many did testify that they were healed by faith during his meetings. An early ministry experience might serve as an explanation of sorts to Roberts' perceived need for an "invalid's tent." Roberts recalled an event in Alton, IL, from his early days in ministry. He said that there he got "a little careless" due to his lack of experience when he encouraged a woman to toss aside her crutches and walk. "Her hands went up and people leaped to their feet rejoicing, and I was standing there thrilled from head to toe." In minutes, the woman crumpled: "like a little bird that had been shot, she just wilted and went down." He pulled her up and the people clapped, but in Roberts's mind, their faith had been diminished. Following that experience, he said that "I became very, very careful from that point on."[183]

---

181 Allen Spraggett, *Kathryn Kuhlman*, 28.

182 Allen Spraggett, *Kathryn Kuhlman*, 28.

183 David Edwin Harrell, Jr., *Oral Roberts: An American Life*, (Bloomington, IN: Indiana University Press, 1985) 83. See also, *Oral Roberts: My Story*, (Tulsa and New York: Summit Book Co., 1961) 134.

It was Roberts' own faith-healing of tuberculosis at the age of sixteen that drew him into the movement, at a time, says Roberts, when the ministry of healing was at a low-ebb in the Pentecostal Holiness denomination where his parents were pastors.[184]

Although some found Roberts to be extreme in his approach to healing, especially in his early tent revivalism days, he was tame compared to others, including A.A. Allen.

A.A. ALLEN (1911–1970)

A faith-healer who may have stirred up the most controversy in the healing revival of the mid-20th century was Asa Alonzo Allen. Spraggett was particularly offended by Allen's style and flamboyant methods. He writes that "My most distasteful experience with a self-styled healer concerned A.A. Allen."[185] He found the promotional materials to be hyperbolic and bordering on fanaticism. The meetings were sold with the promise of "Sight for the Blind!" and "Hearing for the Deaf!"[186] In part, it was also the noise, shouting, and clamor typical of Pentecostal Sawdust Trail worship, commonly referenced as "Old-Time Religion," which was quite popular at the time, that offended his sensibilities. Spraggett describes the healing event he visited:

> The candidate for a miracle, a woman over fifty, in a wheel chair, was said by Allen to have been in a car accident. …

---

184 Vinson Synan, "A Healer in the House? A Historical Perspective On Healing In the Pentecostal/Charismatic Tradition," *AJPS* 3/2 (2000) 189-201, 199. See also, Oral Roberts, *Expect a Miracle: Oral Roberts, an Autobiography*, (Nashville: Thomas Nelson, 1995).

185 Allen Spraggett, *Kathryn Kuhlman*, 30.

186 Allen Spraggett, *Kathryn Kuhlman*, 30.

> "When I lay my hands on you, you're going to feel the power of God go right through you." He clapped his hands to her head and roared at the top of his lungs: "Walk! Walk! Walk! In Jesus' name, I command you to walk."
>
> The woman seemed to be cowed by the thunderous shouts and the evangelist's withering stare; she drew back in the wheel chair.
>
> "Walk! In Jesus' name, walk!" he bellowed again.
>
> This time, assisted by two ushers on either side of her who grasped her firmly by the arms and heaved, the woman tottered to her feet for a few seconds, swayed, and fell back into the wheel chair.
>
> The evangelist solemnly told the congregation that even though the woman was miraculously healed, her muscles had wasted from disuse and would need time to function again... He asked the woman if she had faith that she was healed. She faintly nodded Yes. Then she was wheeled out of the auditorium.[187]

THE BELIEVER'S FAITH

Allen, along with other faith-healers, believed that miracles and healings came as a result of the seeker's faith. Once when praying for a blind coal miner to be healed, Allen shouted an accusation at the congregation: "There is unbelief in this room. I can feel it."[188]

187 Allen Spraggett, *Kathryn Kuhlman*, 32.

188 Roberts Liardon, *God's Generals: Why They Succeeded and Why Some Failed,* (Tulsa, OK: Albury Publishing, 1996) 391. See also, Lexie E. Allen, *God's Man of Faith and Power,* (Hereford, AZ: A.A. Allen Publications, 1954), 106-108.

Allen, born in poverty in Sulphur Rock, Arkansas, in 1911, to an alcoholic father, and a mother who, according to Allen, filled his baby bottle with liquor from the family still, became an alcoholic at an early age. The addiction was never very far from him.[189] Initially ordained by the Assemblies of God, he was defrocked and shunned by the organization after a DWI arrest in Knoxville, TN, from which he forfeited bail and fled the state.[190] When the press attacked him sharply, he told friends that he had been kidnapped and knocked unconscious. When he awoke, he was in a "smoke-filled room and someone was pouring liquor down his throat."[191]

The incident led to his separation from the Assemblies of God. Having been advised to withdraw from ministry for a time, Allen refused and was subsequently defrocked. Organizational officials then warned others in the denomination to shun the evangelist and to "ignore him completely."[192] Nevertheless, the ministry soldiered on.

By the late 1950s, he began to stress financial blessings and became adroit at fundraising based upon faith promises. He claimed that he had learned a scriptural secret to financial success. He related a story of receiving a bill he was unable to pay, having nothing but a few $1 bills in his pocket. Suddenly, the $1 bills were turned into $20s. "I decreed a thing... God said, 'Thou shall

---

189 David Edwin Harrell, Jr., *All Things are Possible: The Healing and Charismatic Revivals in Modern America,* (Bloomington: Indiana University Press, 1975) 66-67.

190 David Edwin Harrell, Jr., *All Things are Possible,* 70.

191 David Edwin Harrell, Jr., *All Things are Possible,* 70.

192 David Edwin Harrell, Jr., *All Things are Possible,* 71. See also, "That the Truth Be Known," *MM* (January 1957), 4-5.

decree a thing, and it shall be established unto thee...' I believe I can command God to perform a miracle for you financially. When you do, God can turn dollar bills into twenties."[193]

Despite the cloud hanging over the ministry, Allen enjoyed the loyalty of a gifted team, including Kent Rogers and R. W. Schambach.[194] Schambach, who left the ministry in 1961 to launch his own successful one, continues to defend Allen against the charges of drunkenness, insisting that he was in the car as witness to the incident and claimed that Allen was not, in fact, drunk, but, rather, was persecuted through the story.[195]

CONCLUSION

The history of American healing revivals and revivalists is one that takes many twists and turns. Kuhlman played an integral part in the era and was as much a part of it as Schambach or Roberts. The Elmer Gantry caricature of the spitting, sweating, screaming tent evangelist was off-putting to the American populace at large throughout the mid-twentieth century. As the revival wound down, the claims became ever more incredible, the volume only grew louder, and the healing revivalists and their boisterous meetings fell increasingly into disrepute. The extreme and often hyperbolic claims tended to offend all but the simplest and neediest of souls. The general populace came to reject and

193 David Edwin Harrell, Jr., *All Things are Possible*, 74-75. See also, A.A. Allen, The Secret to Scriptural Financial Success (Miracle Valley, AZ: A. A. Allen Publications, 1953).

194 David Edwin Harrell, Jr., *All Things are Possible*, 74.

195 Roberts Liardon, *God's Generals*, 400.

even scorn the entire movement as arising from the 'other side of the tracks.'

Kathryn Kuhlman was intimately involved in this world of tent revivalists, first as a young girl accompanying her sister and brother-in-law in their tent revivals, then as God's Girl and later as a young wife, whose duplicitous husband proved himself to be as much of an Elmer Gantry as any. Experiencing such ministry up close had a lasting impact upon her life, an impact that changed her life and future for the better.

CHAPTER FIVE

"Oh, the Blood of Jesus"—Faith and the Atonement

The early pioneers of healing ministry saw physical healing as part of Christ's finished work on the cross. If asked to explain their hope for healing, they might recite to you Isaiah 53: 5, "But he was wounded for our transgressions, he was bruised for our iniquities: the chastisement of our peace was upon him; and with his stripes we are healed," (KJV). The doctrinal understanding is that healing for the body is provided for in the atonement, and it is an ongoing benefit of Christ's deliverance from sin. However, this teaching proved to be a two-edged sword.

On one hand, seekers embrace that power of Christ's death and overcoming victory over sin, seeking to apply it directly to their individual lives. On the other hand, linking one's healing to the atonement might also imply that it was linked to one's own sin. Such a linkage to sin, while valid in certain instances—such as might be the case at times with a disease like syphilis—certainly is not always the case. Nevertheless, linking healing to a seeker's personal sin resulted in a subtle harshness towards those who were already suffering from their illnesses. Ultimately, it was the victim who was to blame or implicated in some way for his or her own sickness.

We see the same question arise in the healing ministry of Jesus Christ, when disciples asked, "Who sinned, this man or his parents?" It was assumed that someone had sinned, thus causing his blindness through their sin. Christ rejected the faulty predicate and redirected everyone's attention to the cure. God in the person of Jesus Christ was present there before them, and he redirected their focus off of sin and blame and onto himself.

> *And as Jesus passed by, he saw a man which was blind from his birth.*
>
> *And his disciples asked him, saying, Master, who did sin, this man, or his parents, that he was born blind? Jesus answered: Neither hath this man sinned, nor his parents: but that the works of God should be made manifest in him.* (John 9:1-2, KJV)

Blame was further meted out upon the revivalists' unhealed supplicants as the power for healing was increasingly understood as the outcome of an individual's faith. In what would eventually end up in a movement of legalism, this lack of faith and suspicion of sin tended to place a heavier burden upon the sick individual than the illness itself.

It was from this tendency to blame the victim for disappointing healing results that Kathryn Kuhlman sought relief, which sent her in earnest pursuit of a new healing theory and methodology. Kuhlman was deeply disturbed by her observations. She said, "I hated traditional tent healing services. Those long healing lines, the filling out of cards... It was an insult to your intelligence. Once, after visiting such a service, I cried all night. I determined that with the Holy Spirit's help, my ministry would not be that way."[196]

SIN AND SICKNESS

As we saw in previous chapters, early Holiness pioneers tended to link healing with salvation as part of the atonement. Rooted in Wesleyan theology, believers in that stream were keen to experience sanctification, or a cleansing from all sin, both past and present, as well as deliverance from the power of sin. The atonement of Christ was received holistically as a cleansing agent for both body and soul. For Wesley, sanctification was not merely positional, but, rather, was an act of deliverance from sin performed by God in the present tense.[197] Although Wesley understood the experience of sanctification as an event impacting the entire person, he did not teach that it was instantaneous. Rather, Wesley saw it as a process of "grace upon grace."[198] Those who followed Wesley took the possibility of liberty from sin and its corruption quite literally and very seriously.

They considered that salvation and sanctification bring rehabilitation from past sins and the resultant corruption, present

196 Hosier, *Kathryn Kuhlman, A Biography*,1977, 66.

197 Kimberly Ervin Alexander, *Pentecostal Healing*, 40.

198 Kimberly Ervin Alexander, *Pentecostal Healing*, 40.

sins, as well as sins committed in the future. The whole person is transformed by the atoning blood of Christ. Gordon saw the atoning work of Christ as two-fold, bringing restoration to both the soul and the body.[199] The inclusion of the body in the atoning work of Christ is highlighted in the declaration of Christ to the infirm man: "And, behold, they brought to him a man sick of the palsy, lying on a bed: and Jesus seeing their faith said unto the sick of the palsy; Son, be of good cheer; thy sins be forgiven thee" (Matt. 9:2, KJV). Another oft-cited passage is found in James 5:14:

> *Is any sick among you? let him call for the elders of the church; and let them pray over him, anointing him with oil in the name of the Lord: And the prayer of faith shall save the sick, and the Lord shall raise him up; and if he have committed sins, they shall be forgiven him.* (KJV)

Read in context of the entire book of James, the word *sick*, which in Greek is κάμνοντα, is better translated "to grow weary" or "to be weary"[200] because the entirety of the book of James deals, not with physical sickness, but with backsliding and discouragement due to the persecution of the times. The standard reading of "physical sickness," and the elders "prayer of faith" is encountered solely in this one instance in the chapter and has endured throughout many generations and translations as the preferred rendering. This reading aided many healing ministry

199 Kimberly Ervin Alexander, *Pentecostal Healing*, 42-43.

200 *Thayer's Greek Lexicon*, Electronic Database. Copyright © 2002, 2003, 2006, 2011 by Biblesoft, Inc. All rights reserved. *BibleSoft.com*, accessed 8/6/2020.

pioneers in establishing a strong link between the two concepts by citing the parallel coupling of *sickness* with personal *sin* ("and if he have committed sins") in James.

According to Kimberly Ervin Alexander, "It is clear from the literature of the movement that its leaders and teachers saw a direct link between sin and sickness (whether specifically or generally as a result of the fall) and that the Atonement provided the deliverance from sin and all of its fallout."[201] The link between sin and sickness, established quite early in the Holiness Movement, would continue as a theological bedrock of healing teaching for generations.

PHOEBE PALMER'S SHORTER WAY

Phoebe Palmer followed Wesley as a theologian and firebrand of the Holiness movement (1807–1874). She believed she found a "shorter way" to holiness and the benefits of sanctification and healing than "this long waiting and struggling with the powers of darkness." "I have thought … whether there is not a *shorter* way of getting this way of holiness than some of our … brethren apprehend?"[202] Palmer believed that the "second blessing" of sanctification that Wesley had taught as a process could be experienced in a moment if one became entirely surrendered to God. In taking this action, i.e., surrendering oneself completely at the altar, Palmer taught that a step of faith would give the assurance of the divine promise. "Phoebe Palmer came to view entire sanctification less as a process than as a state one entered

201 Kimberly Ervin Alexander, *Pentecostal Healing*, 44.

202 Phoebe Palmer, *The Way of Holiness: Notes by the Way*, (Salem, OH: Schmul Publishing Co., Inc.: 1988) 15.

by faith at a definable moment in time."[203] In this "state" the power of sin in the believer's life was broken. According to Alexander, Melvin Dieter has "rightly analyzed that this was a synthesizing of the 'act of faith' and the assurance of faith into one."[204]

CARRIE JUDD MONTGOMERY AND 'RECKONING'

Carrie Judd Montgomery (1858–1946), a disciple of Palmer's Holiness theology, took the teaching a further step, which some would argue was towards *Semi-Pelagianism,* or the development of a personal righteousness based upon one's own works, akin to legalism. Montgomery believed that the power of healing could be found in "reckoning" that the healing was accomplished in Christ historically, and by choosing to exercise one's faith in that truth, the seeker would soon see the desired healing take place. She said, "Our part is very easy, simply to '*reckon*' that this is true because God tells us so; we have no part in the work to do, for that was done for us long ago, and we have only to '*reckon*' that it is done, and done for us individually."[205]

Montgomery's theology of healing shifted the focus from a wrestling in prayer to a deliberate decision to stand in faith on the promises of the Bible. She writes:

---

203 Grant Wacker, *Heaven Below: Early Pentecostals and American Culture,* (Cambridge, MA: Harvard University Press, 2001) 2.

204 Kimberly Ervin Alexander, *Pentecostal Healing,* 45. See also, Melvin Dieter, *The Holiness Revival of the Nineteenth Century* (Metuchen, NJ: Scarecrow, 1996).

205 Carrie Judd Montgomery, "Our Position in Christ," *TOF* 2.1 (Jan. 1882), 1-2. See also H.C. Waddell, "Divine Healing and the Cross," *TOF* 16.4 (Apr 1896), 73-76. See also, Kimberly Ervin Alexander, *Pentecostal Healing,* 45.

> When we have fulfilled, as far as possible, the command given in the fourteenth verse of the fifth chapter of James, we must believe that, according to the Lord's promise, our disease *is* rebuked, and we *are* being made whole. The great point to remember just here is that God's Word is true and we must believe it in spite of every apparent contradiction. These contradictions, if they occur, can be only *seeming* ones, for God is always faithful; but the devil, who is the father of lies, often deceives us into believing feelings and circumstances instead of God's Word.[206]

Montgomery advises those who seek a healing to "believe it [the word] in spite of every contradiction. These contradictions... can be only *seeming* ones..." In other words, she advises seekers to disbelieve what their eyes see and to deny their symptoms. Years later, we encounter similar instructions from Word of Faith evangelist Kenneth Hagin, teaching much the same understanding. He said: "By believing what your physical senses tell you, you would say, 'I don't have healing—I am sick.' But by believing the truth of God's Word you can say, 'I am healed.'"[207] This teaching at the heart of the Positive Confession or Word of Faith Movement is popular today, although we see the seeds of this theology being laid in the late 19th century.

H. Terris Neuman writes: "These statements are in error when compared with the totality of Scripture and their plain

206 Carrie Judd, *The Prayer of Faith,* (Buffalo, NY: The Courier Company, 1880) 93.

207 H. Terris Neumann, "Cultic Origins of Word-Faith Theology Within the Charismatic Movement," *Pneuma: The Journal of the Society for Pentecostal Studies,* Vol. 12, No. 1, Spring 1990, 32-55, 36.

meaning. Nowhere does Jesus Christ or anyone else call sickness a symptom nor is anyone called upon to deny that the sickness is actually present."[208]

Sarah Mix, (Montgomery's mentor) had introduced her to this theory when Montgomery was herself extremely ill. She was encouraged to throw away her medicine and any kind of remedy as an act of consecration.[209] "Now if you can claim that promise, [i.e., James 5:14–15, "the prayer offered in faith will make the sick person well" (NIV)] I have not the least doubt but that you will be healed."[210]

A DIFFERENT WAY TO SEE "FAITH"

One sees in such comments that "faith" has taken on a new focus and has shifted somewhat in its meaning. This shift is important, for we see the new meaning and focus endure for generations and gradually become the foundation for a great deal of misunderstanding and error. Although the sense that an individual would be accepted on his or her own righteousness is rejected in Montgomery's teaching, which was quite a good development, we still see that the foundation seems to be laid, rather completely, for a generation of "hyper-faith" healers. Of faith, Montgomery writes:

> We are apt to regard faith as something high and mysterious, which no one can attain unless born with an unusual degree

208 H. Terris Neumann, "Cultic Origins of Word-Faith Theology Within the Charismatic Movement," 36.

209 Kimberly Ervin Alexander, *Pentecostal Healing*, 46. See also, Carrie Judd, *The Prayer of Faith*, (Buffalo, NY: The Courier Company, 1880), 14.

210 Carrie Judd, *The Prayer of Faith*, 14.

> of it. Some of us are deceived by thinking that great and repeat struggles of mind are necessary in order to secure it, and this idea is pretty strongly rooted, until we really understand the nature of faith. ... Faith is belief, and the question is not how much we must believe God's word, but whether we accept it as true or not true; whether we deem it reliable or not reliable.[211]

In Montgomery we see a focus and exaltation of faith as its own commodity. Faith, or the lack it, clearly is the primary key to receiving a divine healing. That faith begins in the powers of the mind and will, a point that is extremely important in deconstructing the erroneous seeds sown into the stream of faith teachings. It would be these same powers of the mind that would inform, in varying degrees, the healing doctrine of Mary Baker Eddy, E.W. Kenyon, Kenneth Hagin and others.

Montgomery said, "If we take a hold by faith of something we desire, then let go because of doubt, and continue in our indecision, doubt generally conquers, and we let go altogether. Having once laid hold of a promise, by faith, we must *keep hold* of it."[212] In this definition of faith, Montgomery insists upon tenacity and rejection of doubt. Faith itself has become a work, one that replaces the striving towards holiness inherited from previous generations. Once again, faith for Montgomery has become in itself a work and a commodity. *The focus of healing is no longer on the Healer, but on one's own faith: the quality of it, the strength and tenacity of it, and the will and power to reject all doubt.*

211 Carrie Judd, *The Prayer of Faith*, 41.

212 Carrie Judd, *The Prayer of Faith*, 48.

FAITH IN FAITH

This is one of the most important aspects of this erroneous understanding. Faith becomes the entire focus in this process. In a sense, the physically ill are instructed in how to have faith in faith, and not faith in God. The focus has been shifted from God as the center of one's hope for healing, to faith itself as the focus. It is at this point that the teachings begin to diverge from the teachings of the Bible.

Montgomery writes of Mark 9:17-20, the story of the man whose son is possessed by a spirit and appears to be having seizures. Christ admonishes him that "all things are possible to him that believeth." Montgomery interprets this event as follows: "He knew that the only condition was believing, and, without searching his heart to see if he found there some mysterious emotion, such as many people now understand faith to be, he at once signified his willingness to fulfil the necessary condition of *making the effort to believe.*"[213] In these pages we gain a better understanding of Montgomery's definition of faith. "And straightway the father of the child cried out and said, with tears, 'Lord, I believe, help Thou mine unbelief.' … he made the effort of intellect and will, and said, 'Lord, I believe.' … He acted upon the determination to believe in spite of himself, in spite of his unbelief, and *as he made the effort the power was given him.*"[214] The "effort to believe" suggests that the willpower to succeed would come from the seeker. Such teachings throw the ill person into

---

213 Carrie Judd, *The Prayer of Faith*, 52.
214 Carrie Judd, *The Prayer of Faith*, 52-53.

a battle, a struggle of willpower to fight his or her doubts, pain, and perceptions. Part of this struggle of human will that a person entered into would include rejecting any help or comfort from the medical establishment. Like others, Montgomery encouraged seekers to throw away their medicines, believing that "clinging onto medicine implied a lack of faith."[215]

Alexander notates the similarity in theology between Montgomery, Palmer, and Mary Baker Eddy, referencing Raymond Cunningham. While not exploring the matter, she also notes that Dayton affirms this connection as well. Dayton writes:

> A close colleague of Simpson who shared the same ethos was Adoniram Judson Gordon.[216] As pastor of the Clarendon Street Baptist Church in Boston, A.J. Gordon worked out his teachings on healing somewhat more in dialogue with the emerging Christian Science of Mary Baker Eddy, but he clearly shared most features of the Holiness tradition.[217]

Mary Baker Eddy, who began the Christian Science Movement, borrowed heavily from others and "developed an extensive doctrine of the denial of reality. Along with this she added the concept of seeing disease and sickness as merely symptoms and used affirmations as a means of obtaining healing."[218] Since Christian Science is generally considered to be

215 Jennifer A. Miskov, *Life on Wings: The Forgotten Life and Theology of Carrie Judd Montgomery (1858-1946)*, (Cleveland, TN: CPT Press), 148.

216 After whom Gordon College and Seminary in Wenham, MA are named.

217 Donald W. Dayton, *Theological Roots of Pentecostalism*, (Metuchen, NJ: Hendrickson Publishers, Inc., 2007) 128.

218 H. Terris Neumann, "Cultic Origins of Word-Faith Theology Within the Charismatic Movement," 48. See also, James H. Snowden, *The Truth About Christian Science*, (Philadelphia: Westminster Press, 1920) 129.

outside of Christian orthodoxy, we see an enduring influence of genuinely cultic ideas into the early healing movements.[219]

E.W. Kenyon, (1867–1948), although largely overlooked, was the theologian who laid the groundwork for a branch of faith and prosperity teachers and healers who would rise into prominence in America. Scholars generally attribute much of the Word of Faith teaching of Kenneth Hagin and other faith teachers, including Kenneth and Gloria Copeland, to Kenyon. In fact, the lion's share of Hagin's teachings originated with Kenyon.[220]

Kenyon boldly and unapologetically instructed adherents to have "faith in faith." He said, "We become faith men and women, we use faith words, and we produce faith results. 'Faith in my faith.' The first time those words came to me they startled me," he said describing followers who had faith in him instead of themselves. "... the people who ask for prayer haven't confidence in their own faith. For some reason they do not believe in themselves."[221] Notice that Kenyon is instructing followers to believe in "*themselves.*" Here, Kenyon reveals one of the fatal flaws in his understanding. By focusing individuals upon their own faith, they shift their focus from God the healer to themselves and their own resources. The heavy weight placed upon the sick and infirm is increased by, not only the supposed connection between

---

219 Robert S. Ellwood, Jr., *Religious and Spiritual Groups in Modern America* (Englewood Cliffs, NJ: Prentice-Hall, 1973) 80. See also, H. Terris Neumann, "Cultic Origins of Word-Faith Theology Within the Charismatic Movement," 38.

220 See D.R. McConnell, *A Different Gospel: The Cultic Nature of the Modern Faith Movement,* (Peabody, MA: Hendrickson Publishers, 1988, 1995, 2011), 6-14.

221 E.W. Kenyon, *Jesus the Healer,* Kindle Edition. Loc.67.

the seekers and their sin, but also upon their own inability to generate faith within themselves.

THE ROOTS OF THE FAITH HEALING

We have noted that Kuhlman struggled with the theology and praxis of the Sawdust Trail faith healers, which brought her to the breaking point at which she began to seek a better way. It is important to recognize the deep roots of the movement that are outside of orthodoxy, and to understand how widespread this movement's influence was in the early Healing Revivals. While many have dubbed Kenneth Hagin the father of the Faith Movement, a look back reveals that he was something of a latecomer to it. An earlier father of the contemporary movement was E.W. Kenyon. Kenyon's daughter, Ruth Kenyon Houseworth, cried foul over the plagiarism of her father's work: "They've [the Faith teachers] all copied from my Dad. They've changed it a little bit and added their own touch..., but they couldn't change the wording. The Lord gave him words and phrases. He coined them. They can't put it in any other words... It's very difficult for some people to be big enough to give credit to somebody else."[222]

As we have seen, the early links to the Faith Movement date back as far as Montgomery, Cullis, and Baker Eddy, before Pentecostalism and the Charismatic Movement was born. In fact, what was commonly referred to as the "mind-healing" cults were part of the Metaphysical Movement of the early

222 D.R. McConnell, *A Different Gospel: The Cultic Nature of the Modern Faith Movement*, 3.

and mid-19th century.[223] Neuman argues that these teachings are directly related to the early "New Thought" movement in the mid–1800s. "New Thought is a development based on the concepts of Hegel, Emerson, German idealism and New England Transcendentalism.[224]

Mary Baker Eddy (1821–1910), the founder of Christian Science, was deeply influenced by the teachings. "Along with New Thought she sees the cause of disease as mental: 'The cause of all so-called disease is mental, a mortal fear, a mistaken belief or conviction of the necessity and power of ill-health.' Thus, if one is sick his or her thinking is incorrect."[225] Eddy was a student of the father of metaphysical cults: Phineas P. Quimby. A main tenet of this cultish theory is a kind of radical Gnosticism, where it is believed that the only *real* part of a person is his or her spirit being.[226]

Tenets of the theory include an understanding of humans that separates them into three radically distinct and mutually exclusive parts: spirit, soul, and body. The human spirit is a person's fundamental identity and the only means of receiving and understanding revelation knowledge. McConnell charges that Eddy lifted the theory directly from Quimby. Other scholars, including Neuman, Warrington, and others, contend that

223 H. Terris Neumann, "Cultic Origins of Word-Faith Theology Within the Charismatic Movement," 37.

224 H. Terris Neumann, "Cultic Origins of Word-Faith Theology" 38. See also, Robert s. Ellwood, Jr., *Religious and Spiritual Groups in Modern America,* (Englewood Cliffs, NJ: Prentice-Hall, 1973) 80.

225 H. Terris Neumann, "Cultic Origins of Word-Faith Theology Within the Charismatic Movement," 43.

226 D.R McConnell, *A Different Gospel,* 104-105.

Kenyon took the theory from Eddy, and that Kenneth Hagin plagiarized the entire body of teachings directly from Kenyon. The implications concerning the matter are grave, for it suggests that much of the Faith teachings of the early 20th century were sourced in a kind of modern-day Gnosticism related to Christian Science and other mind-cults.[227]

Kenyon taught that only by the human spirit does one communicate with God. Denying the physical senses, i.e. sense knowledge, is a key to faith. The believer who has prayed for healing must deny that the symptoms exist. Kenyon insists that "real faith is acting upon the Word independent of any sense evidence."[228]

An example of sensory denial is found in the doctrine of healing. One's confession must ignore the disease's physical manifestations in the body, which are merely symptoms, and confess that he or she is healed, despite having no change to a condition or illness. "Confession [of faith] always goes ahead of healing," advises Kenyon. "Don't watch symptoms—watch the Word. . . . Don't listen to the senses. Give the Word its place."[229]

> People with Sense Knowledge faith "do not believe they are healed until the pain has left their body." Real faith would

---

227 See H. Terris Neumann, "Cultic Origins of Word-Faith Theology," 32-55, D.R McConnell, *A Different Gospel*, Keith Warrington, "Healing and Kenneth Hagin", AJPS 3/1 (2000), 119-138, and Geir Lee, "The Theology of E.W.. Kenyon: Plan Heresy or Within the Boundaries of Pentecostal-Charismatic 'Orthodoxy'" *Pneuma*, Vol. 22, No. 1, Spring 2000, 85-114.

228 D.R McConnell, *A Different Gospel*, 106.

229 D.R McConnell, *A Different Gospel*, 107. See also, Kenyon, *Jesus the Healer*, 26.

deny the "physical evidence" of pain and listen only to the Word.[230]

This practice of the denial of physical symptoms has been the source of much controversy in the Faith movement.

WORD OF FAITH TEACHINGS

Nevertheless, the purpose of this section is to show that what has become known as the Word of Faith gospel entered the Christian arena far earlier than many have considered, and that it did not originate in Pentecostalism, but, rather, as part of the early Holiness Movement and the Metaphysical Movement. Why is this important? It demonstrates that the tenets of the Word of Faith teachings were quite pervasive and had dramatically influenced the early Pentecostal Healing Revivalists. In fact, when one studies Montgomery, Gordon, Simpson, and others, one discovers that such teachings seeded these movements—teachings that were themselves rooted in cultish ideas connected to Christian Science, New Thought, and the Unity School of Christianity.[231] All of these early metaphysical teachings have been rejected by orthodox Christianity for many years. It is for this reason that we see many practices and teachings that believers might consider to be troubling today. These would include the rejection of medical doctors and medicine, the denial of blatant symptoms, the need to confess what one wants in order to have it occur through the power of words, and to never sabotage

230 McConnell, *A Different Gospel*, 107. See also, Kenyon, *Two Kinds of Faith*, 23.

231 See Neuman, "Cultic Origins."

the process with "negative confessions." Other extra-biblical teachings might include suffering terribly in order to deny the symptoms of a serious illness or disease, and one of the worst teachings and practices, blaming the sick for not being healed.

It's easy to see how, in the context of this history of Faith teachings, that the responsibility fell to the one suffering an illness to make the correct confession, refuse to make the wrong confession, deny one's symptoms and pain, reject medical help, and all the while believing that some sin or offense against God that the sufferer cannot find was the original cause. The burden of faith for obtaining one's healing was placed upon the weak and miserable shoulders of the sufferer, as was the blame for being sick in the first place. It is little wonder that Kathryn Kuhlman, who grew up and became an active participant in the movement from the tender age of 16, who wheeled sufferers into the tents, who watched them leave looking even more miserable and dejected than when they arrived, resolved to find a better way. Regarding this resolution, Kooiman Hosier writes:

> In the early days of her ministry Kathryn was greatly disturbed over many things that she observed in the field of divine healing. Because she was confused by "methods" she saw used and disgusted with "performances" she witnessed.[232]

Healing evangelists often accused the sick individual who went home unhealed following their services with a lack of faith. Kuhlman lamented,

232 Helen Kooiman Hosier, *Kathryn Kuhlman, A Biography*, (London: Lakeland Books, 1977) 66.

> Too often I had seen pathetically sick people dragging their tired, weakened bodies home from a healing service, having been told that they were not healed simply because of their own lack of faith. My heart ached for these people as I knew how they struggled, day after day, trying desperately to obtain *more* faith, taking out that which they had, and trying to analyze it, in a hopeless effort to discover its deficiency which was presumably keeping them from the healing power of God. And I knew their defeat, because they were unwittingly looking at themselves, rather than to God.[233]

BLAMING THE SICK

We see this kind of scolding as far back as Montgomery and farther. Montgomery writes: "A great many people think they never sin, because they do not lie or steal or do something considered dreadful, but perhaps there is no greater sin that one can commit than the sin of unbelief, because it is the foundation of every other sin."[234]

Although faith healers were involved in the process, too often the onus for poor results was borne by the suffering seeker. "To pray the prayer of faith effectively required a great deal from sick persons and the ones ministering to them. The faith of both must be strong. ... Leaders almost always project the blame outward, and the sick usually internalize it."[235]

---

233 Kathryn Kuhlman, *I Believe in Miracles*, (New York: Pyramid Books, 1962) 212.

234 Carrie Judd Montgomery, *Secrets of Victory*, (Oakland, CA: Office of Triumphs of Faith, 1921) 155.

235 Nancy A. Hardesty, *Faith Cure: Divine Healing in the Holiness and Pentecostal Movements*, (Peabody, MA: Hendrickson Publishers, Inc., 2003) 132.

Based upon the understanding that faith was a responsibility of the believer, and that faith itself was akin to a metaphysical force that one must find in his or her own human heart, and based upon the teaching that sickness itself was caused by an individual's sin, blaming the sick for a lack of faith should they not get healed during prayer became the standard procedure. Kuhlman believed in God's power to heal, but crushed by all she witnessed in her tender years, she also knew there must be a better way.

CHAPTER SIX

"They've Taken Away My Lord"

Like other female Pentecostal ministers before her, Kuhlman did not start out with the intention of becoming a healing evangelist. "Like two of her predecessors, Maria Woodworth-Etter and Aimee Semple McPherson, she was a dynamic and successful soul-winner long before she was noted for her healing ministry."[236] The great crowds and opportunities came at the end of a lifetime of evangelism. Kuhlman's ministry falls along two lines: the early years in which she itinerated, reached a crescendo in Denver and fell sharply; and the second part where she reemerged in Franklin, PA, and eventually moved to Pittsburgh. Most people know her from the second half of her ministry. The first half of her ministry, those years most of us have heard less

236 Wayne E. Warner, *Kathryn Kuhlman: The Woman Behind the Miracles*, (Ann Arbor, MI: Servant, 1993), 154.

about, shaped, motivated, and caused her to become the towering ministry figure we see in the second half of her life. It was also in the second half of her lifetime of ministry that the stunning miracles she's come to be identified with began.

It is those miracles, and the way those miracles took place, or the 'method' and/or 'praxis,' that became one of her greatest contributions. The methodology she used and the theological basis for it are some of the most interesting aspects of her incredible life and yet are also what is least understood. Many have attempted to mimic her methods and to adopt her style, but few, if any, have fully understood or appreciated the theological and practical leap she made when she entered into a new realm of spiritual expression. It is this hidden manna that this book seeks to uncover.

HEALING METHODS—THE WHAT AND WHY

Kuhlman discussed her intentional pursuit of more ethical approaches to healing than the ones she had become familiar with to biographer Kooiman Hosier:

> In the early days of her ministry Kathryn was greatly disturbed over many things that she observed in the field of divine healing. "I hated traditional tent healing services," she explained. "...she delved even harder into the Word of God for answers."[237]

237 Helen Kooiman Hosier, *Kathryn Kuhlman, A Biography*, (London: Lakeland Books, 1977), 66.

As a young ministry worker, she had pushed the wheelchairs of tired and defeated believers. She felt they were being blamed because they had "been told that they were not healed simply because of their own lack of faith. My heart ached for these people as I knew how they struggled, day after day, trying desperately to obtain *more* faith, taking out that which they had, and trying to analyze it, in a hopeless effort to discover its deficiency which was presumably keeping them from the healing power of God. And I knew their defeat, because they were unwittingly looking at themselves, rather than to God."[238]

Although historians have suggested that Kuhlman simply visited the healing ministries of noted evangelists in her past, it is clearer from the actual historical record that Kuhlman had become intimately acquainted with the inner-workings of such ministries, first as an assistant to the Parrotts and then in her ministry with Waltrip. No doubt she had pushed the wheelchairs of many defeated and deathly ill individuals out of the tents or buildings and had observed the pain of their disappointment first-hand.

What Kuhlman had experienced in the tent revivals and healing meetings she attended throughout her youth had a crushing impact upon her. "I saw the harm that was being done in attributing everything to 'lack of faith' on the part of the individual who had not received a healing...The looks of despair and disappointment on the faces I had seen, when told that only their lack of faith was keeping them from God, was to haunt me

238 Kathryn Kuhlman, *I Believe in Miracles,* (New York: Pyramid Books, 1962), 212.

for weeks."[239] Emotionally overcome and struggling to find God's compassion in the situation, Kuhlman prayed: "They have taken away my Lord and I know not where they have laid him."[240]

EXPERIENTIAL LOVE

Kuhlman's prayer was answered in the Spring of 1947, when she began studying for a series of sermons on the Holy Spirit. She realized that when the crucified Christ said it was finished, he included not only the salvation of the soul but the healing and deliverance of the body as well. "I knew that if I lived and died and never saw a single healing miracle like the apostles experienced in the book of Acts, it would not change God's Word. He made provision for it in our redemption at Calvary."[241]

Had her theology of healing been formed solely in the sufficiency of the atonement, Kuhlman would not have departed from historical and contemporary thought. However, she went another step in the inclusion of the Holy Spirit. "...Jesus wanted to give His church a gift, the greatest gift possible: the person and the power of the Holy Spirit, the power of the Holy Spirit who was so faithful to Christ's ministry while He was here on earth. The secret in the power and the healing of sick bodies is in the Holy Spirit."[242]

Therefore, although she anchored her theological understanding of the *justification* for healing in the atonement, the *actual* healings themselves would be initiated beyond this

239 Kuhlman, *I Believe in Miracles*, 213.

240 Kuhlman, *I Believe in Miracles*, 213.

241 Buckingham, *Daughter of Destiny*, 102.

242 Kathryn Kuhlman, "The Key—Faith," The Kathryn Kuhlman Foundation, #117, 1979. Radio talk show, audiotape.

doctrinal rationale. She would go another step and anchor her theology in the manifest presence and person of the Holy Spirit. "The secret of the power of the healing of sick bodies is found in the person of the Holy Spirit."[243]

Her revelation of healing did not stop there, however. In addition to identifying the manifested presence of the Holy Spirit as the agency of healing, Kuhlman remarked upon the motivation, which is a vital key. Some may recall that Roberts' and other 'faith' healers' theological foundation for the healing ministry rested purely upon a sufferer's faith access and the atonement doctrine, which Kuhlman rejected. For Kuhlman, the access of faith rested not in an individual's personal beliefs respecting past events (the atonement) but, rather, in Christ's active and experiential love. She explained:

> Love is something you do. The very last thing he did before he went away was to give the Holy Spirit to the church. You can't love without giving. That's the reason he gave the church the greatest possible gift; there is no greater gift than the person who had been so faithful...the one who had not failed him. You shall receive power after that the Holy Ghost comes upon you.[244]

Inspired by the new revelation from her studies, Kuhlman preached a series on the Holy Spirit. After Christ died, he sent the Holy Spirit, the comforter to his church. "The last words he said

243 Kathryn Kuhlman, "The Key—Faith," The Kathryn Kuhlman Foundation, #117, 1979. Radio talk show, audiotape.

244 Kathryn Kuhlman, "Kathryn Kuhlman, Franklin, PA," The Kathryn Kuhlman Foundation, accessed 7/29/2011.

before he went away were, 'And ye shall receive power after that the Holy Ghost is come upon you.'" God the Father had given him the gift, and now he was passing it on to the church. Therefore, every church should be experiencing the same miracles seen at Pentecost. The gift of the Holy Spirit is for us all.[245] The missing piece she had discovered, in Kuhlman's estimation, was the place of the Holy Spirit in the act of healing. The Holy Spirit is the power of the Trinity. It was *His* power which raised Jesus from the dead. It is that *same* resurrection power that flows through our physical bodies today, healing and sanctifying us.[246] As she delivered her revelation about the Holy Spirit that was completely new to her, she shook under the power herself. The next day a woman came up to her and said she had been healed of a cancerous tumor as Kuhlman spoke. She considered this the "beginning of miracles" in her ministry.[247] From 1947 onward her ministry would be characterized by the ministry of healing.[248]

---

245 Buckingham, *Daughter of Destiny*, 104.

246 Kathryn Kuhlman, "The Beginning of Miracles," Kathryn Kuhlman Foundation, n.d.; audiocassette.

247 Kathryn Kuhlman, "The Beginning of Miracles," Kathryn Kuhlman Foundation, n.d.; audiocassette.

248 The cassette recording of Kuhlman's message entitled "The Beginning of Miracles" was one of the most requested, and was the first essay in a posthumous collection of radio messages entitled "*Heart to Heart With Kathryn Kuhlman.*" The story was also printed in a booklet entitled *What Is the Key?* which was published in the early 1960s. This pamphlet was offered during broadcasts of *I Believe in Miracles* free of charge to anyone who requested it by self-addressed stamped envelope. The standard narrative Kuhlman recounted regarding the beginning of miracles in her ministry is contained in these two versions. Kathryn Kuhlman, *What is the Key?* Box 1, Collection 212, The Kathryn Kuhlman Collection, Archives of the Billy Graham Center, Wheaton, IL., in Artman, Amy Collier, "'The Miracle Lady': Kathryn Kuhlman and the Gentrification of Charismatic Christianity in Twentieth-Century America," (PhD diss., The University of Chicago Divinity School, 2009), 65.

WORDS OF HEALING KNOWLEDGE

In time she would announce or "call out" miracles in various sections of her auditoriums and invite long lines of those who felt themselves to be healed to join her on the platform where she would allow them to share their impressions. Some professed that a goiter had suddenly disappeared, others walked out of wheelchairs, still others felt themselves free of cancer.

Customary at Kuhlman services, the evangelist neither formed healing lines for seekers nor laid hands on heads. Instead, she simply declared that a healing was taking place in the seating area in which a seeker was located, a method some call a *word of knowledge* or divinely imparted information regarding the Holy Spirit's healing activity. The individual might attest to experiencing a sensation and some change in symptoms, and therefore would be invited to the platform to share the perception. Later, that person would be advised to seek the confirmation of a medical doctor before medicines or treatments were discontinued. Kuhlman's methodology was adopted by a generation of Pentecostal evangelists and pastors. Kuhlman never berated seekers for their lack of faith, but often cried with them, laughed with them, and marveled at their testimonies.

"WE GIVE YOU PRAISE, LORD JESUS."

A further distinctive of her ministry was the scrupulous effort to return the credit to God. As each and every pilgrim walked across the platform claiming him or herself to be healed, Kuhlman would repeat a mantra: "We give you the praise, Lord Jesus. We give you the praise." During these services she would often stop the proceedings in order to disclaim credit, saying, "I have nothing to do with these healings." "I'm not a healer." "The Holy Ghost has healed you."

Those who walked with her to and from the services claim that this concern only increased after the service was completed. "After a meeting we would be with her and go through the kitchen. I remember her walking through the kitchen and putting her hand out and people would fall down* in the kitchen. In the elevator she would say over and over 'I give it all to you,' [to God] on the way out."[249]

---

* A common occurrence in Kuhlman's meetings was being "slain in the Spirit" or swooning and falling to the ground as they encountered the great manifested presence of God.

249 Telephone interview with Viola Malachuck, conducted 1/29/11.

CHAPTER SEVEN

A Theology of Miracles

Kathryn Kuhlman once joked about the time when she launched out into solo ministry at a very young and tender age with pianist and friend, Helen Gilliford. Her sister Myrtle called her and warned: "Just be sure you are getting your theology straight." Kathryn chortled in the deep throated way that she often did: "I didn't even know what theology was!" [250]

Kuhlman often told audiences that she learned theology only at the feet of Jesus in constant study and prayer. She told of piling on quilts for warmth at the homes of strangers as she attended the Holy Spirit's school of prayer. There she developed her theology by reading the Bible for endless hours and sitting at the feet of the Jesus. "I got my schooling at the feet of the greatest teacher in the world. It wasn't in some great university or theological seminary. It was in the school of prayer under the teaching of the Holy Spirit."[251]

250 Jamie Buckingham, *Daughter of Destiny*, 47.
251 Jamie Buckingham, *Daughter of Destiny*, 47.

THE IMPLICATIONS OF CHRIST'S ATONEMENT

Kuhlman was in agreement with her predecessors in locating her healing theology in the atonement of Christ. But she brought significant differences to even the crux of their claims. Historically, we have seen that the atonement provided the underlayment of the entire movement. According to Alexander, early Holiness teachings as well as the Pentecostal understanding that followed it were both predicated on certain conclusions drawn from their understanding of certain texts.[252] The scriptural promise of restoration based upon the death of Christ on the cross is first found in Isaiah 53:3, "He is despised and rejected of men; a man of sorrows, and acquainted with grief: and we hid as it were our faces from him; he was despised, and we esteemed him not. Surely he hath borne our griefs, and carried our sorrows: yet we did esteem him stricken, smitten of God, and afflicted. But he was wounded for our transgressions, he was bruised for our iniquities: the chastisement of our peace was upon him; and with his stripes we are healed." This same promise is repeated again in Matthew 8:16–17 to show how the promise was fulfilled in the person of Jesus Christ: "When the even was come, they brought unto him many that were possessed with devils: and he cast out the spirits with his word, and healed all that were sick: That it might be fulfilled which was spoken by Esaias the prophet, saying, Himself took our infirmities, and bare our sicknesses." (KJV) The later passage demonstrates that healing indeed was part of the work of Christ on the cross.

Kuhlman joined the company of healing evangelists before her in the anchoring of her hermeneutic, or her scriptural

252 Kimberly Ervin Alexander, *Pentecostal Healing*, 195.

understanding of the basis of healing, in the atonement. However, her agreement stopped there, for it was in the implications of this passage that her subsequent revelation of healing departed sharply from other evangelists.

HEALING AND MIND SCIENCE

We have demonstrated that the teachings on faith that preceded Kuhlman's ministry were largely founded in what Montgomery would have called "reckoning" that a healing had taken place. Once an individual had prayed for his or her healing or had received a prayer from a particular healing evangelist or another minister, that sick individual was then counseled to "reckon" that the healing had taken place. How would this happen? The person would determine in his or her own mind to believe that the healing had taken place, as based upon the Isaiah 53 promise, and then he or she would then reject any physical indicators or "symptoms" to the contrary. By holding onto the word and refusing to believe any contrary physical proofs, the work of faith would begin. Faith healers taught that one needed to deny reality in order to exercise a kind of mind over matter.

Faith healers also asserted that the sick must make the proper "confessions of faith," and the very words they used would command the reality, but a "wrong confession" would sabotage the process and the healing could be lost.

Kuhlman hated the excesses she saw in the ministry field as a young minister, and she hotly rejected the outcomes generated by the theological error that had blanketed much of the whole affair. She confided in her friend, Helen Kooiman Hosier, that the performances she saw only made her delve deeper still into the Word of God for answers.[253] She confided: "I think that no one has ever wanted Truth more avidly than I—nor sought it harder."[254] The looks of despair on the faces of those doubly-burdened souls and their disappointment haunted her. She sobbed out her heart to God as she prayed for understanding.

> Fortunately, I had learned a valuable spiritual lesson early in my ministry—one which was to come to my aid now. I had learned that the only way to get the truth is to come in sincerity and absolute honesty of heart and mind, and let the Lord Himself give one the blessed revelations of His Word, and through the Word, make His Presence real and His Truth known. I waited expectantly for the answer, and it came."[255]

Kuhlman left Denver and headed for Pennsylvania. "Think what a place God chose!" she said. It was the old Billy Sunday Tabernacle where years earlier the famed evangelist had stood preaching with powerful results. The first service brought about a handful of folks, about 38, but in the next two services the building was bustling with people.

> It was in that third service, as I was preaching on the Holy Spirit. Just before I began speaking, a lady stood up and I was shocked when she said, 'Pardon me, Miss Kuhlman, please ... may I give a word of testimony regarding something that happened last evening while you were preaching? While

253 Helen Kooiman Hosier, *Kathryn Kuhlman*, 66.

254 Helen Kooiman Hosier, *Kathryn Kuhlman*, 66-67.

255 Kathryn Kuhlman, *I Believe in Miracles*, (London, Lakeland Paperbacks, 1968), 213. See also, Kooiman Hoiser, *Kathryn Kuhlman*, 67.

> you were preaching on the Holy Ghost, telling us that in Him lay the Resurrection power, I felt the Power of God flow through my body. I knew instantly and definitely that I had been healed. So sure was I of this, that I went to the doctor today and he confirmed that I was healed.' The tumor was gone!"[256]

WHAT HAPPENED?

On the heels of Kuhlman's quest for answers from God, she stumbled upon certain deep and important theological truths that quickly bore dramatic fruit in her ministry, fruit that increased throughout the rest of her career. Kuhlman understood explicitly why the changes happened and what truth had been revealed.

Regrettably, congregations had been instructed to wage a battle against sickness on the wrong battlefront. By looking to themselves, their own willful determination, as well as to other human powers of the mind and speech, those who needed the Lord the most were subtly steered away from the living presence of the Holy Spirit and redirected to the empty and vain human powers. They became human-focused instead of God-focused. The Word of God warns believers that "cursed is the man who trusts in mankind and makes flesh his strength, and whose heart turns away from the Lord," (Jer. 17:5, NASB). Suffering souls, who came to the healing tents believing to meet the Lord during a ministry event, left feeling defeated, demoralized, and farther away from God's healing and comforting presence than when

256 Helen Kooiman Hosier, *Kathryn Kuhlman*, 67.

they arrived. Kuhlman said, "In you and me apart from God there are no ingredients or no qualities that … can create faith."[257]

Kuhlman spoke frankly about faith and the missteps of faith encountered by herself and others who sought to walk in it.

> The more I grow spiritually the more I realize I know practically nothing about faith. All I can tell you is that faith is the quality or that power where those things desired become things possessed. You cannot weigh it or define it to a container. You cannot put your finger on it and positively understand it completely. To try and define it would be like trying to define energy in one comprehensive statement. But although it is not easy to define, we know what it is not. One of the most common errors we make is mistaking faith for presumption. We must constantly be on guard for not mistaking one thing for the other.[258]

HONESTY AND TRUTH

The teachings on healing that Kuhlman rejected created a denial of reality as part of the "right thinking" that they alleged would bring healing. Kuhlman rejected such denial and spoke quite frankly about sickness and its many symptoms. In fact, she assured audiences that while they were living on earth, they would indeed experience sickness as everyone does, even suggesting that she had herself experienced illness. She said, "If you are a part of humanity you will have deep waters. There will be sickness; none of us are immune from disease, and none of us are immune from

257 Kathryn Kuhlman, "The Key – Faith," The Kathryn Kuhlman Foundation, #117, 1979. radio show, audiotape.

258 Kathryn Kuhlman, "The Key—Faith."

heartache." Unlike faith healers whose theological foundation for healing lay in the claim that "every Christian, without exception, should be physically healthy and materially prosperous,[259] and that no believer should make a wrong confession",[260] Kuhlman spoke of illness in terms that were quite the opposite. She said, "You too will know when the night is so dark there's not a star in your sky. His presence will be there with you in the darkness just as surely as his presence will be with you when the sun is shining."[261] Kuhlman encouraged her followers to confront their symptoms and their fears and feelings honestly before the Holy Spirit, casting all of their cares on the One who truly cares about them. She opened the door of grace into God's presence where help and healing could be found reversing decades of denial and shame.

Kuhlman encouraged listeners to her television show in the early 1970s to look to the Holy Spirit's presence for comfort and help during dark times rather than encouraging believers to use the powers of their own minds to try and reject the reality of physical symptoms and sickness.

HEALING MINISTRY SHIFTS

What Kuhlman did was simple but profound: she redirected the focus of the congregants off their diseases, pain, and trouble, off human powers of mind and will, and she refocused their eyes where they should have been all along. "If I wanted to cross a lake,

---

259 See H. Terris Neumann, "Cultic Origins of Word-Faith Theology Within the Charismatic Movement," *Pneuma: The Journal of the Society for Pentecostal Studies*, Vol. 12, No. 1, Spring 1990, 33.

260 See Neumann, "Cultic Origins of Word-Faith Theology," 36.

261 Kathryn Kuhlman, "Relationship with the Holy Spirit," television show, n.d. https://www.youtube.com/watch?v=mfxegUOfrUs. Accessed 9/26/20.

and the only way to cross would be by boat, the sensible thing would be for me to get a boat. It would be most foolish for me to seek the other side of the lake rather than to seek the boat."[262] Gently and compassionately she turned the focus away from the problem and away from themselves, and, with profound ability, brought the needy into the manifest presence and power of the Living God. She shifted the focus to God, the only boat that could take them across, in the person of the Holy Spirit.

THE AGENCY OF HEALING

In so doing, she shifted the agency of healing from the people themselves and their own abilities—their own right thinking, right speaking, resisting of doubt, etc.—to the Holy Spirit. Miracles began as her services lifted the focus to the person of the Holy Spirit. Kuhlman confessed that she taught "the little I knew about the Holy Spirit"[263] in those early Franklin, Pennsylvania services. In time, the services would become a celebration of the Holy Spirit that enveloped her audiences in a glorious presence of God. She shifted the focus away from people, whether in looking to oneself to find an elusive "faith" in the powers of the mind and speech, or the focus on the evangelist.

Bringing audiences into that glorious presence as she redirected the focus became the trademark of her ministry. Service by service, Kuhlman became a maestro conducting a symphony in the Holy Spirit using music, prayer, testimony, and an endless fountain of love in order to lift every eye and heart to

262 Kathryn Kuhlman, "The Key—Faith."

263 Helen Kooiman Hosier, *Kathryn Kuhlman*, 67.

a living God. "Faith is a gift of God; the source of faith, it comes from God and is a gift from God."[264]

No matter what was happening in the lives of her followers, she taught them that the most important thing they could do was to see Jesus, because faith is not found in the powers of the human mind or heart. Jesus Christ *is* our faith: "Don't forget His presence even in the midst of the storm. Jesus says, 'without me you can do nothing.' Why? Because he is our faith."[265]

> If we get our eyes on ourselves, the storm will capsize our boat. Our faith for victory is closer than we know. No person needs to lack faith for the victory as long as they have their eyes on Jesus Christ. He is our faith. He may be asking you the same question that He asked His disciples on that day there was a storm in Galilee, and then Jesus asked one question: Where is your Faith? Somehow in the darkness of this hour, can you hear him asking you the same question? Child of mine, where is your faith? You have struggled so long. Your waters have been so deep. The storm is still raging around. Be quiet and be still. He is asking you the question: Where is your Faith? Your faith is resting in the stern of the boat. Your faith is right there, closer to you than you ever dreamed possible. He is your faith. Feel His wonderful presence, get your eyes off of the storm and off of the circumstances and put your sights on Jesus.[266]

264 Kathryn Kuhlman, "The Key—Faith," The Kathryn Kuhlman Foundation, #117.

265 Kathryn Kuhlman, "The Key—Faith," The Kathryn Kuhlman Foundation, #117.

266 Kathryn Kuhlman, "The Key—Faith," The Kathryn Kuhlman Foundation, #117.

ENTERING IN

How did Kuhlman usher her increasingly enormous crowds into the glorious presence of God service after service without falter or failure? She spoke about certain key revelations—some that quite surprisingly might have resonated more with early church mystics than with the Holiness and Pentecostal healing revivalists of the early 20th century. The techniques she employed for implementing this grand spiritual task will be the topic of discussion the in the following chapters.

CHAPTER EIGHT

Mystical Death

The lights seem to sparkle against her long, mint green dress with flowing long sleeves draped down her thin, upraised arms. She startles the enormous crowd with her statement: "Kathryn Kuhlman died a long time ago. I know the day. I know the hour. I can go to the spot that Kathryn Kuhlman died. You see, for me it was easy, because I had nothing."[267]

The scale and depth of Kuhlman's ministry was predicated upon a pivotal event that occurred early in her career. Although she seldom talked about it, she first spoke in tongues as part of an event she called her "death." "'When I died to self, when I gave Him body, soul, and spirit, He came in and He spoke,' she said. 'It was so deeply moving.'"[268]

---

267 "Kathryn Kuhlman: YouTube: https://www.bing.com/videos/search?q=kathryn+kuhlman+died+I+can+take+you+to+the+spot&docid=608051714385840083&mid=E28BAAE4B61C313B9DC6E28BAAE4B61C313B9DC6&view=detail&FORM =VIRE.

268 Helen Kooiman Hosier, *Kathryn Kuhlman, A Biography*, (London: Lakeland Books, 1977), 136.

She often reflected about this time when she said she died to self and surrendered all to God. Her decision to leave Burroughs Waltrip and live as a single woman for the rest of her life, laying aside her longings for companionship and family, and determining to remain celibate for the purpose of preaching the gospel, was what she referred to when she spoke of "dying." Malachuk, a personal confidante, confirms this observation: "She said when she would speak that Kathryn Kuhlman died. That is what she meant."[269] Kuhlman shared her story in a rare intimate moment:

> I had to make a choice. Would I serve the man I loved or the God I loved? I knew I could not serve God and live with Mister. No one will ever know the pain of dying like I know it, for I loved him more than I loved life itself. And for a time, I loved him even more than God. I finally told him I had to leave. God had never released me from the original call. Not only did I live with him, I had to live with my conscience, and the conviction of the Holy Spirit was almost unbearable. I was tired to trying to justify myself.[270]

That decision became a transcendent one for Kuhlman. Like Abraham was called upon to sacrifice Isaac, Kuhlman would be called upon to prove her devotion to God. Although it surrounded

---

269 Telephone interview with Viola Malachuck, conducted 1/29/11.

270 Sermon by Kathryn Kuhlman, "The Ministry of Healing," delivered at Melodyland, Anaheim, Ca.; Roberts Liardon, *Kathryn Kuhlman, A Spiritual Biography of God's Miracle Working Power*, (Tulsa, Ok.: Harrison House, 1990), 58; provided as an official response to questions by Carol Gray, The Kathryn Kuhlman Foundation, 4411 Stilley Rd., #202, Pittsburgh, Pa, 15227.

one of the greatest controversies of her life, as with Abraham, the event became a doorway through which she entered into a depth of ministry few have crossed.

Millions around the world, Christians and unbelievers alike, attested to the healing virtue displayed in Kuhlman's ministry. Physicians and other medical specialists confirmed hundreds and possibly thousands of miracles, and the multiple thousands turned away at the doors to her services suggest many were convinced that miracles took place.

The dying-to-self experience Kuhlman described regarding events surrounding her marriage to Waltrip were akin to experiences described by mystics who sought to transcend the powers of the present world in order to find a place of operation in the world of the spirit. Spraggett, a secular journalist and psychic researcher, held this opinion.[271] He interviewed Kuhlman for a book on her supernatural power. During the interview she pointing to the day she left Waltrip as the beginning of her Spirit-empowered ministry. She says:

> I remember walking down a dead-end street and realizing that my life was a dead-end street. It was four o'clock in a Saturday afternoon. It was at that time and in that place that I surrendered myself fully to the Holy Spirit. There are some things too sacred to talk about. I will only say that in that moment, with tears streaming down my face, God and I made each other promises. He knows that I'll be true to Him and I know that I'll be true to Him. In that moment,

271 Allen Spraggett, *The Unexplained*, (New York: The American Library, Inc., 1967).

> I yielded to God and obeyed, body, soul, and spirit. I gave him everything.[272]

From the experience she called her "death," Kuhlman pinpointed the beginning of her miracle ministry.

> Then I knew what the scripture meant about taking up your cross. A cross is the symbol of death. That afternoon, Kathryn Kuhlman died. And when I died, God the Holy Spirit came in. There, for the first time, I realized what it meant to have power.[273]

Beyond the practical experience of full surrender and spiritual death, this "mystical death" became a cornerstone of Kuhlman's theological foundation, one which she taught often, albeit without dredging up all the details of her personal failure. Although virtually unschooled in church history, Kuhlman revisited a well-paved path that mystics throughout the centuries had laid. In so doing, she introduced her own folksy version of their theology of the Spirit to modern era Pentecostal thought and praxis. Eventually, other Pentecostals and Charismatics would seek out the teachings of the mystics, but Kuhlman unknowingly went before them, pointing their thirsty souls towards these ancient wells.

Jeanne Guyon, (1648–1717), a noted mystic, described it thus: "To penetrate deeper in the experience of Jesus Christ, it is required that you begin to abandon your whole existence, giving

272 Allen Spraggett, *Kathryn Kuhlman, The Woman Who Believed in Miracles,* (New York: The American Library, Inc., 1970), 114.

273 Allen Spraggett, *Kathryn Kuhlman,* 114.

it up to God."[274] This well describes the depth of abandoned surrender that Kuhlman called her "death."

PRINCIPLES OF PRESENCE

Mystic Thomas A Kempis (1380–1471) taught that dying to self was essential to finding union with God. He said, "My son, said our Lord, forsake thyself, and thou shalt find Me. Stand without following of thine own will, and without all property, and thou shalt profit in grace; and if thou wholly resign thyself into my hand, and take nothing to thee again, thou shalt have the more grace of Me."[275]

Guyon believed that those who would find union with God must let go of everything else: "You must give up both the external and the internal things—all of your concerns must be placed into the hands of God. Forget yourself. Think only of Him. In doing so, your heart will remain free and at peace."[276] She believed that total abandonment, what Kuhlman describes happened on that dead end street, is an essential first step into the depths of Christ. "Abandonment is a matter of the greatest importance if you are to make progress in knowing your Lord. Abandonment is, in fact, the key to the inner court—the key to the fathomless depths. Abandonment is the key to the inward spiritual life."[277]

---

274 Jeanne Guyon, *Experiencing the Depths of Jesus Christ,* (Beaumont, TX: The SeedSowers, n.d.) 32.

275 Thomas A Kempis, trans. Richard Whitford, *The Imitation of Christ,* (New York: Washington Square Press, Inc., 1964) 186.

276 Madame Jeanne Guyon, ed. Donna C. Arthur, *Experiencing God Through Prayer* (Springdale, PA: Whitaker House, 1984) 28.

277 Madame Jeanne Guyon, ed. Donna C. Arthur, *Experiencing God Through Prayer,* (Beaumont, TX: The SeedSowers, n.d.) 33.

Such teachings were not found among the mystics alone; one can find similar accounts among others who have operated in deep and powerful Spiritual ministries. For instance. Andrew Murray (1828–1917), noted revivalist, author, and pastor, renounced all his earthly desire for honor and position. He said, "This was Jesus' goal when He was on earth: 'I seek not mine own honor: I seek the honor of Him that sent me.' In such words we have the keynote of His life.... His intercession in heaven and His promise of an answer to our prayers, Jesus makes His first object the glory of His Father. Is this our object, too? Or are self-interest and self-will the strongest motives urging us to pray?"[278]

Complete obedience was the way Charles G. Finney (1792–1875), American revivalist and pastor, described this "death to self." He said, "To pray effectually you must pray with submission to the will of God. Do not confound submission with indifference. No two things are more unlike each other. ... What I mean by submission in prayer is acquiescence in the revealed will of God. To submit to any command of God is to obey it."[279]

Guyon and others taught that union with God indeed was possible and it can be realized only through death to self, pride, and ambition. Through brokenness, surrender, and "death to self," one can advance to a transcendental state beyond the limitations of the human mind and powers.

Kuhlman reintroduced the possibility of empowerment in this life through union with God, a theme that, although little

278 Andrew Murray, *With Christ in the School of Prayer,* (Springdale, PA: Whitaker House, 1981) 146.

279 Charles G. Finney, ed. Louis Gifford Parkhurst, Jr., *Principles of Prayer,* (Minneapolis, MN: Bethany Fellowship, Inc., 1980) 14.

understood, would become commonly sought in some sectors of Pentecostal/Charismatic thought. Beyond merely teaching that such empowerment exists, Kuhlman inspired a desire for it by demonstrating it in her meetings, which often were transcendent spiritual experiences for her audiences. Her experience of dying to self "...brought with it a kind of self-surrender, a radical selflessness, which she had not felt before."[280] Kuhlman ushered her congregations into the depths of God's presence by paving the way before them. The cost included laying down all she wanted and loved, knew and cared for, and making a vow to Jesus Christ to follow him even to the cross. How much did it cost her? She told us, "It will cost you everything."

280 Allen Spraggett, *Kathryn Kuhlman, The Woman Who Believed in Miracles,* 114.

CHAPTER NINE

"He Touched Me": Experiencing the Holy Spirit

Worship seemed to explode from a great, one-hundred voice choir as thousands of worshippers joined in the chorus. The atmosphere was charged with electricity until a holy hush descended. Blue light reflected off of a frail figure at the center of the platform who spoke in hushed tones.

"This nation needs a fresh baptism of the love of God. So surely before the church is caught up there will be a miracle service or services where literally every person will be healed. I believe that." Kathryn Kuhlman seemed to float across the stage in a long white dress as she shocked the expectant masses with her words:

"You're not here to see Kathryn Kuhlman. I wouldn't walk across the street to see her. She is the most ordinary person you've seen in your life." She nods her head as her eyes seem to glimmer with water and her voice drops lower.

"The only reason God is using the one you are seeing..." she shrugs and starts again: "I was born without talent. I've always had an inferiority complex about my looks. I wasn't even born with hair—just red fuzz on my head. They used to say to Mrs. Kuhlman, 'What a healthy child.'" Kuhlman's light jocularity seems somehow strangely juxtaposed against a contradictory heavy Presence sweeping over the auditorium. Strangely, she seems ready to cry.

"I was born without talent. I used so much of Stillman's freckle cream that my face turned red." She shakes a knowing head and looks up into an expansive ceiling and continues. "One day I said, 'Wonderful Jesus, I don't have a thing. But if you can take nothing and use it, here's nothing. I offer you nothing. I know I love you. All I can give you is my love. I'll give you every ounce of strength in my body.'"

A strange, tangible quiet fills the auditorium. The thousands of seated congregants seem to barely make a sound. Tears splash down from the corners of some of their eyes as music plays softly in the background.

With glistening water visibly filling her eyes, she looks up into the vast empty space of the enormous auditorium seemingly speaking to someone beyond the view of mortal eyes, walks backward and bows: "I've never forgotten from where I've come."

The lights seem to dim and a floodlight reflects sparkling light from her long white dress. "I die a thousand deaths before I walk out on a platform because I know better than anyone else in the whole world that I cannot give it to you. You and I are dependent upon the Holy Ghost. Everything must come through Jesus."

The holy presence is thick, and the congregation seems to barely breathe. Kuhlman's voice gets deeper and quieter: "In this place of worship is the Holy Spirit, the One through whom Jesus offered himself. The Holy Ghost, the mighty third person of the Trinity, moves upon this audience." The word *mooovvees* is stretched long, and Kuhlman draws nearer the crowd and whispers: "In moments like these I feel like being seated, because you don't need me."

The atmosphere seems charged, as the miraculous is on the cusp of exploding in the auditorium. Her final mantra: "We vow before the Holy Spirit to be careful to give you the glory. Forget about Kathryn Kuhlman and focus on Jeeesuuss."[281]

And then it begins, the "calling out" of the miraculous. The music commences and the atmosphere shifts. Soon lines of the healed will form on their way to the platform where they will recount their dramatic experiences.

CHRIST AND THE HOLY SPIRIT

She believed that all of Christ's power to heal was due to the presence of the Holy Spirit. She taught that Christ divested himself of his godly powers in order to walk as a man—what theologians call the *kenosis* or self-emptying of Christ—and that he was just as dependent upon the presence of the Holy Spirit for power as are we his followers.

281 Kathryn Kuhlman, "Dry Land, Living Water," Las Vegas Welcomes Kathryn Kuhlman, May 3, 1975, video recording.

> Jesus is saying it's the same power, the power of the Holy Ghost, the same power that raised Jesus from the dead. Remember that when Jesus walked this earth he was as much man as though he were not God. That was a body of flesh. As much man as though he were not God. He knew the secret of his power; he knew the secret of those miracles. He knew; he understood. That's the reason when he said "ye shall receive that same power." That's something that for years and years I wondered about.[282]

In Kuhlman's theology, the power for healing is found in the manifested presence of God. We witness a similar healing model in Christ's ministry in Luke 5:17 (NASB) "One day He was teaching; and there were some Pharisees and teachers of the law sitting there, who had come from every village of Galilee and Judea and from Jerusalem; and the power of the Lord was present for Him to perform healing." Here, it is noted that the power was present in order for healings to occur. In other words, a special sense of God's manifested presence was notably present. This seems to be the same phenomenon witnessed during the Kuhlman services.

Therefore, although she anchored her understanding of the justification for healing in the atonement, the actual healings themselves would be initiated beyond this doctrinal rationale. She would go another step and anchor her theology in the manifest presence and person of the Holy Spirit. "The secret of the power

---

282 Kathryn Kuhlman, "The Secret to the Power of the Spirit," 1971, https://www.youtube.com/watch?v=yAQlDaEsuY4. Accessed 9/26/20.

of the healing of sick bodies is found in the person of the Holy Spirit,"[283] she said.

After Christ died, he sent the Holy Spirit, the comforter to his church. "The last words he said before he went away were, 'And ye shall receive power after that the Holy Ghost is come upon you." God the Father had given him the gift, and now he was passing it on to the church. Therefore, every church should be experiencing the same miracles seen at Pentecost. The gift of the Holy Spirit is for us all.[284] The missing piece she had discovered, in Kuhlman's estimation, was the place of the Holy Spirit in the act of healing. "The Holy Spirit is the power of the Trinity. It was *His* power which raised Jesus from the dead. It is that same resurrection power that flows through our physical bodies today, healing and sanctifying us."[285]

SPIRITUAL ENCOUNTER: WHEN THE FUTURE BREAKS IN

Kuhlman's theology of healing was based upon spiritual encounter. Consumed and filled with the presence of God through the vital and living person of the Holy Spirit, one enters into a spiritual dimension not tethered by time. Ephesians proclaims that "in Christ" through the presence and power of the Holy Spirit, the believer is, in a sense, transported into the heavenly realm.

---

283 Kathryn Kuhlman, "The Key—Faith," The Kathryn Kuhlman Foundation, #117., n.d.

284 Buckingham, *Daughter of Destiny*, 104.

285 Kathryn Kuhlman, "The Beginning of Miracles," Kathryn Kuhlman Foundation, n.d., audiocassette.

In Ephesians 1:18-2:6, NASB, we find a prayer that explains this incarnational position where Kuhlman took her followers:

> *I pray that the eyes of your heart may be enlightened, so that you will know what is the hope of His calling, what are the riches of the glory of His inheritance in the saints, and what is the surpassing greatness of His power toward us who believe. These are in accordance with the working of the strength of His might which He brought about in Christ, when He raised Him from the dead and seated Him at His right hand in the heavenly places, far above all rule and authority and power and dominion, and every name that is named, not only in this age but also in the one to come. And He put all things in subjection under His feet, and gave Him as head over all things to the church, which is His body, the fullness of Him who fills all in all.*
>
> *And you were dead in your trespasses and sins, in which you formerly walked according to the course of this world, according to the prince of the power of the air, the spirit that is now working in the sons of disobedience. Among them we too all formerly lived in the lusts of our flesh, indulging the desires of the flesh and of the mind, and were by nature children of wrath, even as the rest. But God, being rich in mercy, because of His great love with which He loved us, even when we were dead in our transgressions, made us alive together with Christ* (by grace you have been saved)*, and raised us up with Him, and seated us with Him in the heavenly places in Christ Jesus...*

Believers who are part of the body of Christ are in Christ, "seated with Him in heavenly places," (Eph., 2:6, NASB). The individual becomes keenly aware of this state when he or she experiences the manifested presence of God. In a real sense, the individual has entered the kingdom of God while still remaining in this earthly body. It is in such precious moments of surrendered ecstasy that one steps briefly behind the veil and is permitted to visit a reality that is yet to fully come. Alexander says,

> Wesleyan-Pentecostal theology emphasizes that the Kingdom is inbreaking, and emphasizes a journey toward God, while acknowledging with gratitude what has already been accomplished. This enables its adherents to hold together the tension between *already* and the *not yet.*[286]

In other words, in the manifested presence of God, the believer steps into the future kingdom, a redeemed millennial world that has not yet arrived, while at the same time eagerly waiting for it in this present world. Christ came preaching the kingdom of God had come, because there in his presence was the kingdom. When the believer becomes keenly aware of that state of being "in Christ" in the present tense, he or she also becomes aware of a kingdom that is yet to come. This is the theology of encounter, one that Kuhlman demonstrated through her life and was especially gifted to bring others into along with her. In a sense, she brought other believers into her own prayer closet, and there, together with her they experienced an amazing Presence that was but a foretaste of the kingdom which is to come.

During the Azusa revival, the earliest Pentecostals experienced a similar "in-breaking" presence of God that was accompanied by

286 Kimberly Ervin Alexander, *Pentecostal Healing*, 241.

healings and miracles. Such are the "signs"[287] of the future kingdom of God or the *eschatos.* Harvey Cox says, "The early Pentecostals saw themselves as positioned 'between the already and the not-yet,' as witnesses to the 'first fruits of the Kingdom' but not yet to its fullness, living in the light that precedes the dawn."[288] This "encounter" with the Holy Spirit was not only for those privileged to enter into the depths of God in such truly wonderful ways, but they considered their testimonies as having unique meaning and import for the entire world.[289] Christ taught that the breaking in of the future—the kingdom of God—meant that those who were hungry and thirsty for God would be given access.

> *And He answered and said to them, "Go and report to John what you have seen and heard: the blind receive sight, the lame walk, the lepers are cleansed, and the deaf hear, the dead are raised up, the poor have the gospel preached to them."* (Luke 7:22, NASB)

"Not only did early Pentecostals believe that the Kingdom of God was coming soon, they also believed they themselves were the evidence of its arrival," says Cox. "The future was already breaking into the present. ... Healing and tongues and prophesies were seen as certain signs of the imminent arrival of the reign of the King."[290] Kuhlman often spoke of the presence of God that 'broke into' her meetings as a "foretaste." In so doing, she

287 See Mark 16:16-18.

288 Harvey Cox, *Fire From Heaven: The Rise of Pentecostal Spirituality and the Reshaping of Religion in the Twenty-First Century,* (Reading, MA: Addison-Wesley Publishing Company, 1995) 316.

289 Harvey Cox, *Fire From Heaven,* 316.

290 Harvey Cox, *Fire From Heaven,* 317.

acknowledged this same sense of being positioned between the 'already' and the 'not-yet' of the kingdom of God or the *eschatos.*

Kuhlman describes how it felt to her in those moments of breaking in as "ecstasy."[291] Paul Tillich notes that *ecstasy* is not an irrational state, but rather "a way of knowing that transcends everyday awareness, one in which 'deep speaks to deep.'"[292] Cox, a student of Tillich, says, "At some level, if only in dreams, nearly everyone longs for such an experience."[293]

Steven Land sees the tension between the 'already and not-yet' of the coming kingdom of God as fueling a deep sense of passion. He says, "This 'promise-fulfilment, already—not yet' is a tensed dynamic which characterizes Christianity's eschatological passion."[294] It is in this in-between '*neither-land*' that healing takes place. "Healing was in anticipation of the final healing of all things. The material was meant for the spiritual and vice-versa. Healing anticipated a millennial restoration of all things: heaven come to earth and no more sickness or sorrow."[295] In discussing great moves of the Holy Spirit—of which this author might include the Kuhlman services—a predominant feature is an awakening of the sense of God's coming kingdom. Peter Althouse notes of Land that "movements of spiritual awakening, revival and renewal, such as

291 Kathryn Kuhlman, "Full Gospel Businessmen's Fellowship," Logos International; videocassette, n.d.

292 Harvey Cox, *Fire From Heaven*, 86.

293 Harvey Cox, *Fire From Heaven*, 86.

294 Steven Jack Land, *Pentecostal Spirituality: A Passion for the Kingdom*, (Cleveland, TN: CPT Press, 2010) 3.

295 Steven Jack Land, *Pentecostal Spirituality*, 45.

the Pentecostal Movement, are the catalyst that kept the tension between the 'already' and the 'not yet' from being resolved."[296]

In Land's perspective, this place of tension created a heart-cry in believers. "Already the Bride was being prepared; already hearts were filled with 'rapture' as they labored, watched and prayed. The faith, worldview, experience, and practice of Pentecostals were thoroughly eschatological. They lived within the tension of the already but not yet consummated kingdom."[297]

It is out of this passion for the presence that we find explanation for Kuhlman's unusual weeping. She attempts to describe her longing for God as she stands before her congregation pleading: "Please don't grieve the Holy Spirit. He's all I've got."[298]

THE COMING KINGDOM

Many Pentecostals and Charismatics seem a bit uncomfortable with the earlier preoccupation of Spirit-filled believers with the coming millennial kingdom, but Kuhlman was quite focused on it in her teachings and commented on it often. The coming kingdom of God, or eschatological concerns, were never far from Kuhlman's thoughts. She preached often of these events throughout her life, and especially during the second part of her ministry after she left Denver. Rather than discomfort, she seemed very much aware of a kingdom that was coming soon.

296 Peter Althouse, "Revisioning Pentecostal Eschatology: Contemporary Pentecostal Theologians Rethink the Kingdom of God," *Spirit of the Last Days: Pentecostal Eschatology in Conversation with Jürgen Moltmann,* (NY: T&T Clark International, 2003) 61-66, 65.

297 Steven Jack Land, *Pentecostal Spirituality*, 46.

298 As recounted often by Benny Hinn. See also, Benny Hinn, *Good Morning Holy Spirit,* (Nashville: Thomas Nelson, 1919) 9.

> If I told you that an hour will come when the president is not elected you would call me a fake. Don't minimize the United States of America. I am proud that I am an American. But the nations are crumbling. Something is happening. The nations are on a chessboard and world affairs are shaping up. ... God has hooks in the jaws of the nations.[299]

As far back as 1949, she heralded the eschatological message:

> Men and women are streaming in large numbers through the gates of Zion. I say to you we are living in the last days. The Holy Spirit will soon leave this old earth when we have the rapture of the church.[300]

Such a preoccupation with the coming of Christ's kingdom is shared, not only with early Christians, but with many others who appear to live quite close to God's presence. For early Pentecostals, the coming kingdom seemed very near, and their focus on eschatological events was central to their entire belief structure. "The physical, literal return of Jesus to the earth is an important feature of Pentecostal spirituality, Menzies describing it as 'a key to history' as a result of which 'God will bring His plan to its glorious fulfillment' (see 2 Pet. 3:3–10)."[301]

---

299 Kathryn Kuhlman, "Dry Land, Living Water," Las Vegas Welcomes Kathryn Kuhlman, May 3, 1975, video recording.

300 Kathryn Kuhlman, Sermon, April 19, 1949 (Tuesday morning). Transcribed early daily teachings and sermons. The Flower Center.

301 Keith Warrington, *Pentecostal Theology: A Theology of Encounter*, (London: T&T Clark, 2008) 313.

A THEOLOGICAL TIGHTWIRE

Kuhlman seemed to balance with ease the tension between the two constructs of the 'already' but 'not yet' reality. Some have complained that the spiritually minded are sometimes of "no earthly good." Those focused on the millennial kingdom can develop a disregard for the current needs of people whose lives are full of injustice, poverty, need and discrimination. Others seem to care little about the care of the earth that God entrusted to Adam and Eve (see Gen. 1:26). Many lives tipped off balance on this highwire between spiritual and natural concerns, but Kuhlman's did not.

While maintaining a wholesale dependence upon the kingdom of God and its dramatic foretaste of an eternal kingdom, she continued to pour into many social "earth-bound" concerns. Kuhlman used the considerable sums of wealth collected from the offerings of great crowds to fund through her foundation an impressive list of philanthropic endeavors. Till her death, she took $25,000 annually as a salary [302]and used what was not plowed back into her television costs to fund these many independent outreaches. That is not to say she did not enjoy her life, for her friend Malachuk indicates that she had beautiful clothes and other costly items at her modest Fox Chapel home.[303]

TAKE NOT THY HOLY SPIRIT FROM ME

"I know what David meant when he said, 'Take not thy Holy Spirit from me.' I probably know better than anyone in this place,

302 "Kathryn Kuhlman, Evangelist and Faith Healer Dies in Tulsa," *The New York Times*, Feb. 22, 1976.

303 Telephone interview with Viola Malachuck, conducted 1/29/11

what he meant and how he felt. I'm not afraid of Satan. I can use the same weapon on Satan that Jesus did: 'It is written.' I fear no man. I have but one fear: lest I grieve the Holy Spirit, lest this anointing shall leave." Kuhlman spoke to a chapel filled with young ministry students.[304]

"Yesterday, the thousands in this arena only saw the miracles, only saw the glory. But very few could see the price that was paid before those miracles took place." Turning her watery eyes upward, her voice deepened, "He can take everything that I've got, but take not thy Holy Spirit from me. I'm willing to live on bread and water for the rest of my life, so help me God. I'll preach it if I have to preach it from a street corner."[305] Her body was frail and thin but her voice strong and resolute. In a few short years, a heart condition would take her life, and the nearness of that date with eternity seemed to impassion the seriousness in her voice.

Kuhlman's life and ministry were a celebration of the Holy Spirit, and those who attended her meetings and watched her on television gained a new respect and understanding of the third person of the Trinity. She seemed to know the Holy Spirit more personally and with greater depth and insight than other prominent Christian figures. "I know the secret of the power in my own ministry," Kuhlman points a long finger into the television camera.

Kuhlman's meetings, especially in the last phases of her ministry, might have seemed odd to the Pentecostal believer who expected shouting and clapping, or to the Charismatic Christian

---

304 Kathryn Kuhlman, "The Secret to the Power of the Spirit," 1971, https://www.youtube.com/watch?v=yAQlDaEsuY4. Accessed 9/26/20.

305 Kathryn Kuhlman, "The Secret to the Power of the Spirit," 1971, https://www.youtube.com/watch?v=yAQlDaEsuY4. Accessed 9/26/20.

who came to expect teachings on the baptism of the Holy Spirit and to hear the gift of speaking in tongues in operation. Much of the time spent in the long meetings involved Kuhlman sharing and talking, usually extemporaneously, as she waited for the presence of the Holy Spirit to sweep into the service and perform miracles. She often chided in her signature good-natured jocularity that "if the Holy Spirit doesn't show up, I'm sunk!"

THE BAPTISM OF THE HOLY SPIRIT

Raised on the Pentecostal Sawdust Trail, schooled at the feet of Pentecostal masters such as McPherson and Simpson, and widely lauded by the Charismatic Movement that swept North America in the mid-century, Kuhlman was rarely benefitted by the embrace of any group. In fact, her practical theology was truly her own, as was her ministry's Pentecostal praxis and tone.

"Kuhlman suffered from the fact that she walked in a theological shadow world between the Pentecostal and mainline Protestant denominations. The Pentecostals held her at arm's length. On the one hand, she did make a distinction between professing Christ and accepting the gift of the Holy Spirit, thus implying the two-stage process characteristic of classical Pentecostalism. However, at least by the 1940s, she did not preach the necessity of a 'second Baptism,' thus denying one of Pentecostalism's central tenets."[306] According to Fredrick Jordan, Kuhlman did not teach the baptism of the Holy Spirit as a second

306 Fredrick W. Jordan, "At Arm's Length: The First Presbyterian Church, Pittsburgh, and Kathryn Kuhlman"; Edith L. Blumhofer, Russell Spittler, and Grant A. Wacker, eds. *Pentecostal Currents in American Protestantism,* (Urbana and Chicago: University of Illinois Press, 1999), 189.

experience in the early years of her ministry. However, although she seldom emphasized it in her sermons, other biographers such as Buckingham, trace a long relationship with the doctrine from the earliest years of her ministry.[307] In fact, she readily acknowledges having had the experience, but in the early 1970s when the Charismatic Movement was at its height, and everyone seemed focused on the experience, her lack of similar singular focus created a question in the minds of her audiences.

THE UNHEALED

Kuhlman claimed to be completely detached from the process of healing, which was why she took no credit for them. She also took no credit for the disappointment when an individual did not get healed. She believed that a day would come when everyone would be healed who attended a particular service, but it never occurred during her life and ministry.

Because the healings were contingent upon the Holy Spirit breaking into the current realm in time, no healing or miracle could be assumed. However, she also believed she needed to cooperate with the Holy Spirit to help facilitate the process.

Like most people, Kuhlman simply saw sickness and disease as part of the human condition. She said, "If you are a part of humanity you will have deep waters. There will be sickness. If you are a part of humanity, none of us are immune from sickness. None of us are immune from heartache.[308]

---

307 Buckingham, 44.

308 Kathryn Kuhlman, "Relationship With the Holy Spirit", *I Believe In Miracles,* television show recording. n.d. https://www.youtube.com/watch?v=mfxegUOfrUs.

CHAPTER TEN

Kathryn Kuhlman the Mystic?

In charting the young Kuhlman's journey across the American heartland, remarkable features were included in her repertoire of homespun stories and vignettes, but were not found in any other contemporary camp. In searching for parallel experiences to hers, one finds himself or herself revisiting the well-chronicled journeys of the mystics.

Bernard McGinn considered that "mystical elements" have been present in Christianity from its very origins. He said that the goal of mysticism "may be conceived of as a particular kind of encounter between God and the human, between the Infinite Spirit and the finite human spirit..."[309] This is one of the most interesting aspects of this unusual woman, and one that holds

309 Bernard McGinn, *The Foundations of Mysticism: Origins to the Fifth Century*, (NY: The Crossroad Publishing Company, 1992) xvi.

important keys for understanding her as well as accessing the dynamic knowledge of the Holy One that she apparently possessed.

Kuhlman was largely unschooled, and from time to time spoke about her lack of formal education. She had dropped out of high school after the tenth grade.[310] Although she added some Bible schooling beyond that, she never admitted to it, preferring to project her dependency upon the Holy Spirit in her private studies. She said, "I haven't had an education; I don't have anything to fall back on. I lean completely on Him (the Holy Spirit), and all that I know He's taught me. I don't know anything else. He's my teacher, and He's been my teacher all of these years."[311] It might be said that this classroom of the Holy Spirit she attended led her to a place that was surprisingly similar to that of history's mystics.

It was the early church mystics who wrote about experiencing a "mystical death," or a complete and a total abandonment of self to God along with all the possessions and pleasures that this life affords. When one consults Spiritual Theology and historical Western Christian Mysticism, he or she discovers greater insight into the many unusual spiritual occurrences Kuhlman and her audiences report so often. In fact, the parallels are so interesting and enlightening that exploring them holds important insight for the believer who desires to go deeper in God. The rest of this chapter is devoted to these interesting and insightful parallels. The first spiritual phenomenon is deep weeping.

---

310 Warner, 47.

311 Kathryn Kuhlman, "The Secret to the Power of the Spirit," 1971, https://www.youtube.com/watch?v=yAQlDaEsuY4. Accessed 9/26/20.

WEEPING IN INTERCESSORY PRAYER

Her stunned audience sat in near total stillness as the wet faced woman behind the pulpit wept and sobbed into the microphone: "Please don't grieve the Holy Spirit. Please, don't grieve him."[312] Kathryn Kuhlman cried openly while her audience sat quietly, barely breathing.

The weeping, although unusual in Pentecostal circles, was in previous times seen as a movement of deep intercessory prayer. Kuhlman noted it in one of her talks: "You come into the service and you weep, but you don't know why you weep. It's the presence of the Holy Spirit that makes you weep," she explained.[313] Kuhlman introduced spiritual concepts that were wholly novel to worshippers, many of whom were more accustomed to formal denominational services or the boisterous clapping and stomping, singing, eruptions of glossolalia, and shouting experienced in the healing ministries of the Pentecostalism of the Sawdust Trail.

SILENCE BEFORE GOD

One regular attendee recounted another dramatic movement of the Holy Spirit during a Kuhlman service with the introduction of complete silence. Although commonly experienced by Roman Catholics in worship, the attendees at a particular service consisted of boisterous Jamaican Pentecostals known for jubilant clapping, dancing, and even shouting. Nevertheless, Kuhlman drew her crowd to a complete hush. When a man continued to

---

312 As recounted often by Benny Hinn. See also, Benny Hinn, *Good Morning Holy Spirit*, (Nashville: Thomas Nelson, 1919) 9.

313 Kathryn Kuhlman, "I Believe in Miracles," television show. https://www.youtube.com/watch?v=tCnEX3a5IBM. Accessed 9/26/2020.

murmur in tongues under his breath, she spoke to him directly from the pulpit, demanding absolute silence. Her obstreperous crowd complied for endless minutes of utter silence, eventually broken by numerous individuals around the room being slain in the Spirit and dropping to the floor.[314] The phenomenon of being *slain in the Spirit*, experienced quite early in Kuhlman's ministry, was brought to the public fore by Kuhlman, who during times of special "visitation" saw entire sections of an auditorium of hundreds at a time undergo the experience simultaneously without so much as a touch from her.

Mystic Teresa of Avila, in her work *The Way of Perfection* taught that as one reaches higher levels of union with God that silent prayer increases, until "ritual and language are completely sidetracked in the process of silent contemplation and spiritual uplifting."[315] According to Teresa, the more an individual prays, the more intimate that one becomes with God.[316]

DARK NIGHTS OF THE SOUL

Beyond the mystical death she notes so often in her sermons, she also endured a long season of mystical progress, called by St. John of the Cross "the dark night of the soul." Kuhlman found herself on a desert of spiritual drought for several years following her departure from Waltrip. According to St. John of the Cross, in this phenomenon "the soul is progressing through the beginner

314 An experience recounted by Benny Hinn.

315 Joseph Dan, 1995 "The Language of Mystical Prayer," *Studies in Spirituality* 5: 40—60, 48.

316 Simon Chan, *Spiritual Theology: A Systematic Study of the Christian Life*, (Downer's Grove. Ill: InterVarsity Press, 1998) 128.

to proficient stage. Once the soul passes through, one experiences a deeper kind of joy and the spirit of love."[317]

LOVE FROM ABOVE

Kuhlman's revelation of healing did not stop at the shift in focus from "faith" to the manifested presence of the Holy Spirit. In addition to identifying the manifested presence of the Holy Spirit as the agency of healing, Kuhlman remarked upon the motivation, which is a vital key. Some may recall that Roberts and other "faith" healers' theological foundation for the healing ministry rested purely upon a sufferer's faith access and the atonement doctrine, which Kuhlman rejected. For Kuhlman, the access of faith rested not in a doctrinal understanding but in Christ's love.

Agapē or "selfless love" was one of the most important terms of early history of Christian mysticism.[318] Another notable shift that Kuhlman brought to healing ministry was in its motivation, where the animator or impetus for healing was shifted by Kuhlman also from 'faith' to love. Whereas the tent revivalists taught a transactional faith exchange brought healing, one that was largely based in the powers of the seeker's mind and will, as the sick individual worked furiously to gain healing through a formulaic endeavor, now everything changed. Rather than the seeker bringing faith into an exchange, now the individual enters into the divine presence where he or she receives a gift that is the loving benefit of a willing God. Kuhlman, through a charism of the Spirit, would call out or speak out the healings

317 Simon Chan, *Spiritual Theology: A Systematic Study of the Christian Life*, (Downer's Grove. Ill: InterVarsity Press, 1998) 135.

318 Bernard McGinn, *The Foundations of Mysticism*, 72.

that were taking place in the room. No hands were laid, no faith work transacted, no yelling and shaking, all would change and an entirely new atmosphere of worship was created with music and prayer.

ECSTASY AND ALTERED STATES

The apostle Paul rehearses an experience that altered his sense of consciousness and caused him to question what kind of spiritual moment it was. He said: "I know a man in Christ who fourteen years ago—whether in the body I do not know, or out of the body I do not know, God knows—such a man was caught up to the third heaven" (2 Cor. 12:2, NASB). The apostle shared this altered state with others who would come much later in time, including the ancient mystics and possibly even Kathryn Kuhlman.

Kuhlman's meetings were transcendent spiritual experiences for her audiences in which...... God became so real to her that the mundane world receded into a relative unreality. The immediacy of her perception of God was so overpowering that at times she felt it was God controlling her body, not she herself.[319] She preached about her spiritual perceptions, which some have called "out-of-body" experiences, although she referred to her altered state as "ecstasy."[320] "There is evidence of dissociation, or trance, in Kathryn Kuhlman's ministry. She said that during the miracle services she often is 'in the Spirit'—a state or condition which she describes as 'being out of the body.' She is unaware of her

319 Allen Spraggett, *Kathryn Kuhlman, The Woman Who Believed in Miracles*, 114.
320 Kathryn Kuhlman, "Full Gospel Businessmen's Fellowship," *Logos International*; videocassette, n.d.

surroundings or herself while in this condition."[321] Regarding this experience, Kuhlman said, "Please realize how detached I feel from the things that happen [in the services]. That is the reason why it never fazes me when the miracles and ministry are discredited, because it isn't me. I am completely detached,' she said.'"[322] "It's as if my body is possessed by the Holy Spirit and as though I were removed, up above somewhere, looking down on the proceedings. I feel as though I am just a bystander. And to tell the truth, I am honestly just as amazed as anyone else by the miracles. And I know that I have absolutely nothing to do with it."[323]

Christian mystics in the early church spoke of similar impressions of altered states of reality. McGinn explains the common characteristics that mark the mystic and his or her expressions of encounter and divine presence: "Mystics continue to affirm that their mode of access to God is radically different from that found in ordinary consciousness, even from the awareness of God gained through the usual religious activities of prayer, sacraments, and other rituals."[324]

Kuhlman indicated that her sense of 'self' is completely laid aside, and that she feels utterly detached and disconnected from the miracles and healings, as if she is but one more member of the audience. "My poor old mottled tongue doesn't have the ability to tell you what I feel about the Holy Spirit. I know better

---

321 Allen Spraggett, *The Unexplained*, 165.

322 Hosier, 75.

323 Kathryn Kuhlman, "Full Gospel Businessmen's Fellowship," *Logos International*; videocassette, n.d.

324 Bernard McGinn, *The Foundations of Mysticism*, xix.

than anyone else the secret of this ministry. Nothing you could say would flatter me. I tell you very frankly, Kathryn Kuhlman is so completely detached from that which is happening in this ministry because it's not Kathryn Kuhlman. It's the power of the Holy Ghost."[325]

The Bible says that it is 'Not by might, nor by power, but by my Spirit, saith the Lord,' and that is the only explanation.'"[326]

> This out-of-body experience ... is the altered state of consciousness in which Kathryn Kuhlman is caught up in a mystic rapture. This is the ecstasy in which I have seen her, at times, stand for several minutes, in what appears to be a cataleptic state, her face upturned, her hands outstretched in prayer, unmoving, transfixed, in ethereal smile on her lips. She seems oblivious of her surroundings, in a transport of wonder and of joy.[327]

Kuhlman called the feeling she experienced "ecstasy"[328] but nevertheless struggled to find the words to express her sense of encounter. Even the inability to articulate such experiences is commonly expressed by mystics. The ways in which individuals through the ages have expressed their experiences of encounter with God's presence are many, but most agree that the experiences defy explanation. "Among the other major mystical categories

325 Kathryn Kuhlman, "The Secret to the Power of the Spirit," 1971, https://www.youtube.com/watch?v=yAQlDaEsuY4. Accessed 9/26/20.

326 Hosier, 76.

327 Allen Spraggett, *Kathryn Kuhlman, The Woman Who Believed in Miracles*, (New York: The American Library, Inc., 1970), 114.

328 Kathryn Kuhlman, "Full Gospel Businessmen's Fellowship," Logos International; videocassette, n.d.

are those of contemplation and the vision of God, deification, the birth of the Word in the soul, ecstasy, even perhaps radical obedience to the present divine will. All of these can be conceived of as different but complementary ways of presenting the consciousness of direct presence."[329]

DENIAL OF SELF WITH DISARMING HUMILITY

It also may have been her death-to-self experience that left her with such disarming humility. She once told a massive crowd that they had not come to see Kathryn Kuhlman. She said she would not walk across the street to see Kathryn Kuhlman, and neither would they.[330] On other occasions she spoke of her earlier life by saying that no one wanted to hear a girl evangelist speak, and she couldn't blame them. She had a unique ability to shift the focus of her audiences away from herself and onto God. In every service, she protested continually that she had no power to heal anyone, that only God had the power to heal. She refused to even claim a gift, saying that if God were so gracious to give anyone a gift, that person should not speak of it. It is in this scrupulous reverence that she helped her audiences to enter into their own transcendent experiences with the Holy Spirit.

This sense of losing oneself and finding God in divine union harkens back to the early mystics, who would have understood

329 Bernard McGinn, *The Foundations of Mysticism: Origins to the Fifth Century,* (NY: The Crossroad Publishing Company, 1992) xvii.

330 Kathryn Kuhlman, "Dry Land, Living Water," Las Vegas Welcomes Kathryn Kuhlman, May 3, 1975, video recording.

better what Kuhlman was attempting to explain. She once declared loudly as she preached to an enormous crowd that "He doesn't want less of me and more of Thee. He wants none of me and all of Thee!"

Kuhlman often referred to herself as "nothing." She would say that she prayed to God that if He could "take nothing, here's nothing." "All I have to give him is my love."[331] Such self-deprecation is unheard of from most pulpits and shocks the sensibilities of the listener upon the first hearing of it. Some hearing this oft-repeated refrain from Kuhlman might conclude that she had extremely low self-esteem or was simply working too hard to feign humility. Jürgen Moltmann says, "The mysticism of everyday life is probably the most profound mysticism of all; the acceptance of the lowliness of one's own life is the true humility, and simple existence is life in God."[332]

When one seeks to understand the access Kuhlman had to the depths of God's presence, a different picture begins to form. An essential goal of the early mystic was a sense of complete union with God and a loss of self, wherein self became "nothing." McGinn says, "This goal, essential characteristic, or defining note has most often been seen as the experience of some form of union with God, particularly a union of absorption for identity

---

331 See Kathryn Kuhlman, "Faith," Kathryn Kuhlman Foundation, T5 #212, c. 1950s. radio talk, audiocassette. See also Kathryn Kuhlman, "Beginning of Miracles," Kathryn Kuhlman Foundation, K832, n.d., audiocassette. This is an oft-repeated refrain that can be accessed in many of her recordings.

332 Jürgen Moltmann, *The Spirit of Life: A Universal Affirmation*, (Minneapolis, MN: Fortress Press, 1992) 211.

in which the individual personality is lost."[333] In other words, the one united with God in that presence experiences a sense that self is "nothing" and that God is everything. Moltmann says, "There is no longer any Nothingness to threaten creation. For in God the Nothingness is annihilated and 'immortal being' has been manifested. So because of God's cross, creation already lives from God, and will be transformed in God."[334]

Kuhlman spoke of a state she would enter that provides additional meaning and understanding. She said, "There is a place where everything is yielded completely."[335] This author believes she was speaking of a state of being, the same state described by Spraggett as "altered."[336] In an interview about the supernatural she gave to Spraggett, she called this place or state "in the Spirit."

> She said that during the miracle services she often is "in the Spirit"—a state or condition which she describes as "being out of the body." She is unaware of her surroundings or herself while in this condition. The rapture may last as long as ten minutes at a time. Members of the congregation told me that when the evangelist is in rapture they often see strange lights playing about her head. One woman said she had seen Jesus stand at Miss Kuhlman's side. Another devout woman reported seeing the evangelist transfigured into a likeness of Christ.[337]

---

333 Bernard McGinn, *The Foundations of Mysticism*, xvi.

334 Jürgen Moltmann, *The Spirit of Life*, 213.

335 Kathryn Kuhlman, "An Hour with Kathryn Kuhlman," Kathryn Kuhlman Foundation, n.d. audiocassette.

336 Allen Spraggett, *The Unexplained*, 165.

337 Allen Spraggett, *The Unexplained*, 164.

ABIDING PRAYER: PRAYER WITHOUT CEASING

Kuhlman, whose theology of miracles changed the Pentecostal/ Charismatic Movements and presented them with an entirely new praxis of healing, also largely reshaped its understanding of prayer. Hitherto, since the days of the Azusa revival, classical Pentecostal prayer had been a loud and boisterous affair, noted by dramatic eruptions of glossolalia, shouting, running, and other outward displays. Kuhlman, in contrast, was often attacked by her more traditional Pentecostal detractors because her prayer and devotional life departed from these norms.

More than once Kuhlman was blasted by critics for what appeared to be the lack of a regular prayer and devotional time. It was one of the questions most often asked of her during interviews, one she seemed to struggle to explain. She told her followers that she stayed prayed up, that she was always in prayer, but none seemed to understand what she was attempting to convey. Close friend and confidante, Maggie Hartner, said, "I've worked with Kathryn for years. Kathryn Kuhlman is praying all the time."[338]

David Wilkerson recalls Kuhlman telling him that, "'I take my secret closet with me—if I'm in a car that's my secret closet, or where I am—there's nothing in the Bible about being in a geographical place or location to pray—I've learned to commune with the Lord anytime anyplace.' This is but one of the many great spiritual lessons Kathryn Kuhlman taught me to pray without ceasing."[339] Practicing the presence of God, an askesis

338 Hosier, 73.

339 Hosier, 73.

forgotten from the days of monk Brother Lawrence and mystics like Jean Pierre de Caussade, was re-introduced into Pentecostal and Charismatic devotion in some measure through the praxis of Kuhlman.

Simon Chan suggests that prayer in union with God is less produced by the emotionalism of old-time Pentecostalism and more by the practice of entering into the ongoing prayer of the Trinity, wherein Christ "ever liveth to make intercession." "The whole life of a Christian may be described as a life of prayer. The life of prayer is embodied in Paul's injunction to pray without ceasing."[340] With great simplicity Kuhlman re-laid a foundation of prayer and spiritual union long lost to the time of monks and mystics. Through displays of great spiritual visitation and power she demonstrated without theoretical exegesis the benefit of her life of spiritual union with God. *Time Magazine* in 1970 called her a "one-woman shrine of Lourdes," a phrase that stuck as press and public, believer and skeptic, acknowledged that her life was unusually touched by a spiritual presence.[341]

Kuhlman said, "A reporter once said to me, 'How much time do you spend preparing for a miracle service?' The question threw me at the time because it was the very first time it had been asked. I said to him, 'You don't understand, *I stay prepared.* You don't prepare for a service [like this], *I'm prepared twenty-four hours out of the day.*"[342]

---

340 Chan, 127.

341 Buckingham, *Daughter of Destiny*, 224.

342 Hosier, 73.

"I VOW, I VOW"

In every great service and immediately before the miracles and healings took place, Kathryn Kuhlman repeated a mantra of sorts. She would end her prayer with a vow: "We vow before the Holy Spirit to be careful to give you the glory."[343] This vow she repeated at each and every service always directly preceded the outpouring of power and the operation of the gift.

It appears to be a renewal of a vow she made during the time of consecration she calls her "death." She said at that time she and God had made sacred promises to one another, promises too sacred to share. It seems that each time she vowed to give God the honor, glory and praise at the onset of miracles, she was repeating, at least in part, that sacred vow.

At one service before a ballroom filled with people she shared a bit more than what was normal. She prayed as follows:

> Father, I stand here and I renew every vow that I've ever made to you. Father, I go back to Twin Falls, Idaho, and that old blue bedspread, the old blue walls, and the old blue worn carpet where I made some vows that day. And I've tried to keep them the best I could. Vows that only you and I know, and I stand here all over again this Saturday afternoon all over again, and I renew every vow and every promise I ever made to you. And whether it's for a day or two days or for a week, as long as there is breath in my body and as long as you keep this old heart beating, I vow to give you every

343 Kathryn Kuhlman, "Dry Land, Living Water," Las Vegas Welcomes Kathryn Kuhlman, May 3, 1975, video recording.

ounce of strength that there is in my body. When I stand in your presence, I know already what I'm going to say. When I see you face to face, I know already what I'm going to say: Dear Jesus. I tried. I didn't do a perfect job, but it isn't because I didn't want to. It's because I didn't know any better. But I tried.[344]

344 Kathryn Kuhlman, "The Secret To The Power Of Holy Spirit" n.d. audio tape. https://www.youtube.com/watch?v=HIsOf1O7u64.

CHAPTER ELEVEN

There's Room for All: Passing the Torch

Kathryn Kuhlman told her audiences many times that "He is not looking for golden vessels. He is not looking for silver vessels. He is looking for yielded vessels." She whispered in hushed tones as if she was sharing a deeply guarded secret: "When you learn this secret, when you understand the person and presence and power of the Holy Spirit being with us, it will be the easiest thing in the world for you to pray and receive your healing from Him, to receive anything from Him."[345] She seemingly wanted to pass the torch of healing to her faithful crowds.

Kuhlman appeared increasingly frail and thin at her appearances throughout the early-mid 1970s. At a gathering of students at the Oral Roberts University chapel, she again seemed to be passing the torch: "Young people, I really do not believe

345 Kathryn Kuhlman, "The Secret to the Power of the Spirit, 1971. https://www.youtube.com/watch?v=yAQlDaEsuY4. Accessed 9/26/20.

that God has given me something special. Young people, I'll tell you what I really believe. God has not given to me one thing that he will not give to anyone of you if you'll pay the price. I'm not special to him. There isn't one thing that he has done through me that he will not do through you," she paused and straightened up her withered back and looked directly into their eyes, "if you'll pay the price."[346] She seemed to choke away tears as her eyes shone with water:

> I would lie if I was to tell you the price was cheap. Everybody is out for a bargain these days, but God has no bargains. You see me walk out there on stage, and all you see is the glamour of it. There's a price. And it depends on what you want most.[347]

In time, other well-known ministers like Pat Robertson and Carlton Pearson would begin calling out healings after her method. Following her untimely death in 1976, large ministries would lay claim to her disciples and methods. But none seemed to truly understand or practice the depths of her love and devotion to both God and people.

PASSING THE TORCH OF PASSION FOR THE POOR

Kuhlman's ministry extended beyond the healing services and television spots to an area that she never spoke about, the benevolence to the poor. In fact, much of Kuhlman's early

346 Kathryn Kuhlman, "Knowing the Spirit," ORU Chapel 1972, video. https://www.youtube.com/watch?v=FMMVWN1BBUs. Accessed 9/20/20.

347 Kathryn Kuhlman, "Knowing the Spirit," ORU Chapel 1972, video.

ministry efforts were directed towards a preponderance of blue-collar workers who comprised the Rust Belt's middle and lower-middle-classes, and the poor, outcast, and disenfranchised. As the ministry gained wider acceptance, the upper-echelons of society embraced Kuhlman. But, initially and for most of her years of service, Kuhlman was a darling of simple folk: the uneducated, hardworking people who may have seen their lives reflected in her folksy vignettes.

Benevolence efforts were an integral part of the Kuhlman ministry from its earliest days during the Depression Era when the Denver Tabernacle formed a commissary to reach out to people who lacked food.[348] At the height of her ministry, although she never erected a building or launched her own denomination, her foundation underwrote the funding of many outreach ministries, programs, and charitable efforts.

Those ministry efforts continued on long after her death through the Kathryn Kuhlman Foundation well into the 21st century.

PASSING THE ECUMENICAL TORCH

From the earliest days of her ministry, Kuhlman bridged denominations and presented a spiritual ecumenism that provided a wide platform of Pentecostal expression. Wayne Warner said that "at the grass-roots of mainstream Protestant and Catholic churches she brought people together, poured balm into their religious wounds, and shaped opinions and practices as an ecumenist and Evangelical-Pentecostal ambassador—although she described her

348 Warner, 194.

ministry as one who simply carried 'a water bucket for the Lord,' and as a 'handmaiden of the Lord.'"[349] Her ecumenical vision predates the Charismatic Renewal that embraced her. In Denver, 1935, she pleaded for religious unity:

> We've tried working up revivals; we have exhausted ourselves programming and planning 'em; looks like we're going to have to get back to the old-fashioned methods of Wesley, Finney, Spurgeon, and Moody—praying them down. When revivals are prayed down God gets the glory; when man tries to work them up, it doesn't work. Might as well try to make a lily or a rose. Let's forget our doctrinal differences, shall we? Let's unite in earnest prayer that God will visit Denver with a glorious super-natural revival of old-time religion; that folks will be really 'born again,' and then lives will be changed, and broken homes reunited, and sorrows turned into joys.[350]

PASSING THE TORCH TO YOUNG WOMEN MINISTERS

Possibly as a response to rising subordinationists and a rising resistance to female leaders, Kuhlman seldom spoke on the subject of women in ministry. She shared that she sometimes wished she had not been called and had remained a farm wife in Missouri with a man to "boss her around."[351] Uncharacteristically, she once

349 Wayne Warner, "At the Grass-Roots: Kathryn Kuhlman's Pentecostal-Charismatic Influence on Mainstream Churches," *Pneuma: The Journal of the Society for Pentecostal Studies,* Vol. 17, No. 1, Spring 1995, 51-65, 51.

350 Kathryn Kuhlman, March 10, 1935, "Tabernacle Joy Bells" (courtesy Western History Collection, Denver Public Library).

351 Kathryn Kuhlman, "An Hour with Kathryn Kuhlman", audiocassette.

declared that women have much more courage than men, but she always spoke of men in the most respectful of terms. In her folksy talks, she would often describe a man who worked hard to provide for his family or the care of a father for an ailing child.

Although the ranks of female ministers dropped precipitously during the era, Kuhlman's ministry remained relatively unaffected, which can be attributed to the transcendent quality of her ministry, which was difficult even for her detractors to deny. That her ministry continued to grow against the backdrop of increasing limitations upon women ministers is a tribute to her. Kuhlman generally asked audiences to not see her as a woman in ministry, but to think of her only as a servant of the Lord. Only once did Kuhlman rise up and aggressively defend herself as a female minister.

A CLASH WITH MALE MINISTERS

The one junction at which her ministry hotly clashed with the subordinationist currents of the time was over the 1976 World Conference of the Holy Spirit in Jerusalem. She was scheduled as the keynote speaker, and Logos International president, Dan Malachuck, who organized the event, also invited Bob Mumford, a noted "Shepherding"[352] teacher, to speak, as well. In a move that

352 Charismatics shifted towards authoritarianism and strict gender hierarchism as leaders such as Christenson reinterpreted the movement in authoritarian terms. Books including *The Christian Family* became standard fodder and an exaggerated authoritarianism reached a crescendo as leaders emerged teaching a slavish subjugation to spiritual leaders called the Shepherding Movement. "Covering" teachings proliferated in a kind of Ponzi pyramid structure that introduced significant spiritual abuse into the young Christian community predominated by new

was completely out of character for her, she threatened to cancel her appearance if the 'Shepherding' minister was not disinvited. She flatly refused to minister at the same conference. Kuhlman was reported as announcing, "If Bob Mumford goes to Israel, I shall not go. That man is a heretic…I shall not appear on the same platform with him."[353] She may have suspected that he would have challenged her right to speak as a female, which, considering the tenor of the times, might have occurred.

"It was in November, 1976, and we arranged to have a film done," said Viola Malachuk, wife of the late Dan Malachuk. "She said she wouldn't go on with Bob Mumford. They were against everything she was doing, and she was very adamant that she

---

converts. "Each layperson was submitted to another pastor in a kind of chain of command with a senior or presiding pastor overseeing a local church network of pastors." Estimates of as many as 50,000 adherents were directly related to the movement at its peak in 1982 with 500 associated churches. Its monthly magazine New Wine, was distributed to more than 110,000 subscribers reaching 140 nations. See Don Basham, "Forum: CGM and New Wine," *New Wine*, (December 1976, 31. See also David. S. Moore, *Shepherding Movement* (Journal of Pentecostal Theology), (London: T&T Clark International, 2003) 6. Women were especially targeted by the teachings, and coupled with increasing interest in demonology, female leadership, which became the target of suspicion in many circles, was rejected as arising from a "Jezebel spirit." Such notions continued to shape the movement long into the 1980s after many shepherding leaders and followers had renounced the error. Early Women's Aglow meetings stressed female subordination and domesticity, with many churches and leaders permitting women to meet only with a male attendant to "cover" the women in the meeting. See R. Marie Grifith, "A 'Network of Praying Women': Women's Aglow Fellowship and Mainline American Protestantism," 131-151, *Pentecostal Currents in American Protestantism*, eds. Edith L. Blumbhofer, et al., (Chicago: University of Illinois Press, 1999); Charles Simpson, "Covering of the Lord," *New Wine*, (Dec. 1974,) 28- 31.

353 David. S. Moore, *Shepherding Movement (Journal of Pentecostal Theology)*, (London: T&T Clark International, 2003) 111.

wouldn't be there with that. Dan had already planned to have a film done of her, and it was all lined up."

The Malachuks had a long-time relationship with Mumford that predated his involvement in the Shepherding Movement. In response to Kuhlman's demand, Logos International retracted the invitation. "We felt bad because of our personal relationship with Bob. Dan had invited him. At first the Shepherding guys were involved with FGBMF, but their involvement cooled. We didn't think the Shepherding Movement was a very good idea either."[354]

Kuhlman's response to the Shepherding teachers created negative reverberations throughout the Charismatic community. Following the event, Viola tried to contact Mumford to discuss some updates on one of his books, but was unable to speak with him. "They wouldn't let me talk to him because of the whole thing. It was not very well received in a lot of circles."

In time, some of the Shepherding teachers would publicly repent for disseminating teachings that ultimately harmed the body of Christ. Such teachings had helped to erect a stained-glass ceiling against female ministers that has not been fully dismantled.

---

354 Telephone interview with Viola Malachuck, conducted 1/29/11.

CHAPTER TWELVE

In Conclusion

The nurse who attended Kathryn Kuhlman at her death on February 20, 1976 shared an unusual experience. As Miss Kuhlman quietly passed into glory, a fragrance of roses filled the room. The nurse said, "The absolute warmest, thickest, most overwhelming smell of roses absolutely flooded the room."[355] When a supervisor arrived from an adjacent building she exclaimed: "Oh, this is where the smell is coming from. I could smell it on 3 East." The nurse continued, she could "smell it in the other part of the building that was on the other side of the four-lane road."[356]

Interestingly, when sacrifices were offered to the Lord in the Hebrew Temple, the Bible often says they brought forth a "sweet

355 "How Kathryn Kuhlman Died. She Said She Saw Jesus Coming. A Story by the nurse who attended to her." Jun 1, 2019; https://www.youtube.com/watch?v=ggldmPY8qJs.

356 "How Kathryn Kuhlman Died." Jun 1, 2019.

smelling aroma" to the Lord. For instance, Exodus 29:18 reads as follows:

> *You shall offer up in smoke the whole ram on the altar; it is a burnt offering to the Lord: it is a soothing aroma, an offering by fire to the Lord.* (NASB)

It seems that in this last and final miracle of her life, God was attesting from heaven that this sacrificed life of Kathryn Kuhlman, one that was completely surrendered and passionately filled with the Holy Spirit, had brought to God a sweet aroma. This author believes that God was pleased with her life of passionate love and total surrender. Ephesians 5:2 encourages all believers to "walk in love, just as Christ also loved you and gave Himself up for us, an offering and a sacrifice to God as a fragrant aroma" (Phil. 4:18, NASB). Although she stumbled and fell, struggled and tried, in the end she triumphed. She was honored by the one she loved most of all:

> *But thanks be to God, who always leads us in triumph in Christ, and manifests through us the sweet aroma of the knowledge of Him in every place. For we are a fragrance of Christ to God among those who are being saved and among those who are perishing.*
> (2 Cor. 2:14–15, NASB)

THE LEGACY OF A LIFE WELL LIVED

Kathryn Kuhlman leaves to us all a legacy of struggle and triumph, of standing alone against a world of pressures and difficulties, with one goal and focus: to see and know her God and to bring others to the same knowledge.

In a day and time when the injustices of racism had risen to a crescendo that finally reached a climax in social upheaval, when long cultivated seeds of inequality and discrimination seemed to tear at the fabric of society, when the American Christian community was fragmented from centuries of strife and division, Kuhlman rose to prominence with transcendent spirituality, self-deprecating humor, and disarming humility. At a time when women acquiesced to cultural pressures and internal doubts, when the public mood had shifted radically away from the receptivity of females in the pulpit, and when significant numbers of called women were abandoning Christian service for the comforts of home and family, she answered the call. Her commitment to the poor and needy never changed, but rather went on for many decades after her death.

Kuhlman was a Joshua who took sick and needy into the promised land of genuine hope and healing virtue: into the liberty of the Holy Spirit. She demonstrated a transcendent faith that not only promised the presence of the Spirit, but that ushered her congregations of nuns and priests, atheists and sinners, rich and poor, popular and obscure into the very depths of the presence of God.

She rose to heights of prominence seldom reached by ministers during the Charismatic Revival of the late 20th century. Her ministry was distinctly ecumenical. Often she could look out to crowds of priests in collars and nuns in habits, the working poor in common attire, and a sprinkling into the mix of celebrities, politicians, and movie stars. Although divorced, a state very much frowned upon in an era with increasingly limited opportunities for women ministers, she found ways to transcend this hurdle and other challenges largely through her disarming humility and unquestionable ministry results. She won the hearts of the press, which has not happened before or since.

She moved the often rowdy Pentecostal prayer experience into the secret place and brought down the volume. In so doing, they began to widen the circle of traditional Christians who felt comfortable embracing charisms of the Spirit. She single-handedly changed healing theology and praxis for generations of believers. Kuhlman shaped a Pentecostal/Charismatic expression that reached across denominational boundaries, paving the way for an ecumenical cross-referencing of many forms, including its worship and emphasis on spiritual gifts.

Her gatherings demonstrated egalitarian features and led the culture in the promotion of racial and gender inclusion, despite increasing shifts in US culture towards segregation and gender bias. Kuhlman's ministries reached out to many races and cultures and offered young women a noteworthy example of love and success.

In practice, her organization was uniquely characterized by a deep and genuine love for the unchurched, broken, outcast, poor, and infirm displayed through a variety of ongoing support mechanisms. Yet, Kuhlman never lost her passion for reaching the lost.

Her greatest achievement, however, was in re-visioning healing theology and praxis by reframing the focus upon God, as well as reintroducing long forgotten ancient pathways of mystical prayer and spirituality. Today, she continues to be celebrated as a truly unique and genuine servant of God.

Bibliography

"A Gift of Healing," review of *Kathryn Kuhlman: The Woman Behind the Miracles,* by Wayne E. Warner, Christian Century. August 2-9, 1995. 748-752.

Alexander, Kimberly Ervin, *Pentecostal Healing: Models in Theology and Practice.* Blanford Forum, Dorset UK: Deo Publishing, 2006.

Althouse, Peter, *Spirit of the Last Days: Pentecostal Eschatology in Conversation with Jürgen Moltmann.* NY: T&T Clark International, 2003.

"An Examination of Kingdom, Dominion, and Latter Rain Theology: Franklin Hall." Dr. Waltrip ("Kathryn Kuhlman's husband") last surfaced in ministry with Franklin Hall in 1946 where he helped establish a prayer and fasting center in San Diego.; *Apologetics Index,* websource: http://www.apologeticsindex.org/106.html.

Anderson, Allan. *An Introduction to Pentecostalism.* Cambridge, UK: Cambridge University Press, 2004.

"Annual Study Reveals America is Spiritually Stagnant." *Barna.* March 5, 2001. websource: http://www.barna.org/barna-update/article/5-barna-update/37-annual-study-reveals; accessed 7/22/2011.

Artman, Amy Collier, "'The Miracle Lady': Kathryn Kuhlman and the Gentrification of Charismatic Christianity in Twentieth-Century America." PhD diss., The University of Chicago Divinity School, 2009.

Artman, Amy Collier. *The Miracle Lady: Kathryn Kuhlman ad the Transformation of Charismatic Christianity.* Grand Rapids, MI: William B. Eerdmans Publishing Co., 2019.

Bayles, Ronald L., "Minister's Wife Healed of Lymphoma." *The Pentecostal Evangel.* June 12, 1977.

Blumhofer, Edith L. "Women in American Pentecostalism." *Pneuma.* Vol 17, Number 1, Spring 1995.

__________. "Women in Pentecostalism." *Union Seminary Quarterly Review 57.* 2003: 101–122.

Bridge Johns, Cheryl, *Pentecostal Formation, A Pedagogy Among the Oppressed*, eds. Thomas, John Christopher, Moore, Rick D., Land, Steven J. Eugene, OR: Wipf & Stock, 1998.

Buckingham, Jamie, *Daughter of Destiny*. South Plainfield, NJ: Bridge Publishing, 1976.

Burroughs Waltrip III, the grandson of Burroughs Waltrip, writes: "...He left and wrote two short books. He then became a sales man selling concrete liners for caskets. That was in Kansas City, MO or KS. That is the last our family has been able to discover. He is my grandfather, and I would like to know what happened to him."

Carnegie Hall, North Side, Pgh. PA, newspaper photo of standing room only crowd regularly lining up from early morning for services. Thursday, June 16, 1949.

Catholic Encyclopedia, 1912, "Woman." This article addresses the Roman Catholic theological perspective of women in the early twentieth century. Such views were widely prevalent in many religious groups.

Chan, Simon. *Spiritual Theology: A Systematic Study of the Christian Life*. Downer's Grove. Ill: InterVarsity Press, 1998.

"Chartered Bus to Kathryn Kuhlman Services, Friday, Nov. 11; Bus stops in Connellsville, Mt. Pleasant, Youngwood and Greensburg," *The Daily Courier, Connellsville, PA*. Wednesday, November 9, 1966.

Coulter, Dale M. "What Meaneth This? Pentecostals and Theological Inquiry." Lee University, School of Religion, Cleveland, TN, 2001.

Cox, Harvey, *Fire from Heaven, The Rise of Pentecostal Spirituality and the Reshaping of Religion in the Twenty-First Century*. Reading, MA: Addison-Wesley Publishing Company, 1995.

Cox, Harvey. "A Review of *Pentecostal Spirituality: A Passion for the Kingdom*, by Steven J. Land. *JPT* 5. 1994. 3–12.

Cunningham, Loren, and Hamilton, David Joel. *Why Not Women?* Seattle, WA: YWAM Publishing, 2000.

Dart, John. "Evangelist Kuhlman's Jewelry to be Sold. *Los Angeles Times*. May 2, 1998.

Daugherty, Billy Joe. *101 Days of Absolute Surrender*. Tulsa, OK: Harrison House Publishers, 2006. excerpted at *cfaith.com*; http://cfaith.com/index.php?view; accessed: 10/23/2010; Quote: "On January 8, 1981, I was praying about where our church could meet when it suddenly became crystal clear: 'Tink Wilkerson's Auto Mart.'"

Dayton, Donald W. *Theological Roots of Pentecostalism.* Metuchen, NJ: Baker Academic, 2007.

Death Certificate of Emma Kuhlman. April 8, 1957.

Death Certificate of Joseph H. Kuhlman. December 30, 1934.

Decatur Bible College. *Summit Yearbook.* 1926. 27.

de Alminana, Margaret English. "Reconnecting with the Mystics: Kathryn Kuhlman and the Reshaping of Early Pentecostalism." *The Journal of the European Pentecostal Theological Association,* vol. 33.1, 2013.

de Alminana, Margaret English and Olena, Lois E., eds. *Women in Pentecostal and Charismatic Ministry: Informing an Ongoing Gender-Focused Dialogue on the Faith Contributions of Women.* Global Pentecostal and Charismatic Studies Series. Leiden: Brill, 2016.

de Alminana, Margaret English. "A Biographical Survey of 20th Century Female Pentecostal Leadership and an Incipient Egalitarian Struggle," Ph.D. diss., Glyndŵr University, U.K., 2011.

English (de Alminana), Margaret, *Removing the Veil.* Jacksonville: Bridge-Logos, 2008.

"Evangelist Adds $3036 to Fund: Capacity Rally Donates for Crippled Children." November 1948 news article.

Everts, Janet Meyer. "Brokenness as the Center of a Woman's Ministry," *Pneuma, the Journal for the Society of Pentecostal Studies.* Vol. 17, No. 2, Fall 1995.

Farah, Charles. *Faith or Presumption?: From the Pinnacle of the Temple.* Plainfield, NJ: Logos International, n.d.

Faupel, William D. *The Everlasting Gospel: The Significance of Eschatology in the Development of Pentecostal Though.* Sheffield, UK: Sheffield Academic Press, 1996.

Fee, Gordon D. *The Disease of the Health and Wealth Gospels.* Vancouver, BC: Regent College Publishing, 2006.

Finney Charles G., ed. Parkhurst, Louis Gifford, Jr. *Principles of Prayer.* Minneapolis, MN: Bethany Fellowship, Inc., 1980.

"Four Years of Donations Built $120 Million Hospital of Faith." *New York Times.* Oct. 20, 1981.

Gill, Deborah M. "Ripe for Decision: Women-In-Ministry Issues of Century 21." *Enrichment Journal.* Assemblies of God USA) 3/31/06 <. http://enrichmentjournal.ag.org/200102/040_ripe_for_decision.cfm>.

Gilley, Gary E. "'Pentecostalism' *Think on these Things.*" Southern View Chapel, Springfield, IL, 1999) 2.; <http://www.rapidnet.com/`jbeard/bm/Psychology/char/more/pente.htm>.

Goll, Michal Ann. *A Call to the Secret Place.* Shippensburg, PA: Destiny Image, 2002.

Goss, Don. H., Rev. Rector of St. Peter's Episcopal Church, Brentwood. "Through Kathryn Kuhlman's Ministry...A Physician Is Healed." *The Pittsburgher.* n.d.)

Grady, J. Lee. "Where are the Women of Fire? What American Women Can Learn from Female Leaders in China, Russia and Africa." Fall 2003< http://cbeinternational.org>.

Grenz, Stanley J., and Muir Kjesbo, Denise. *Women in the Church.* Downers Grove, IL: InterVarsity Press, 1995.

Guyon, Madame Jeanne, ed. Arthur, Donna C. *Experiencing God Through Prayer.* Springdale, PA: Whitaker House, 1984.

Hammack, Mary L. *A Dictionary of Women in Church History.* Chicago, IL: Moody Press, 1984.

Hardesty, Nancy A. *Faith Cure: Divine Healing in the Holiness and Pentecostal Movements.* Peabody, MA: Hendrickson Publishers, Inc., 2003.

Harrell, Jr., David Edwin. *All Things Are Possible: The Healing and Charismatic Revivals in Modern America.* Bloomington, IN: Indiana University Press, 1975.

______ *Oral Roberts: An American Life.* Bloomington, IN: Indiana University Press, 1985.

"Healing and Revival: US—Colorado Listings." *HealingandRevival.com.* websource: http://www.healingandrevival.com/USCO.html., accessed 1/1/2011.

Hildebrand, Lloyd. interview and correspondence, 10/15/10 and 1/18/10.

Hosier, Helen Kooiman. *Kathryn Kuhlman, A Biography.* London: Lakeland Books, 1977.

Jacobsen, Douglass. *A Reader in Pentecostal Theology: Voices from the First Generation.* Bloomington, IN: Indiana University Press, 2006.

Kartsonakis, Dino, with Murphey, Cecil. *Dino, Beyond the Glitz and Glamour, An Autobiography.* Nashville: Thomas Nelson Publishing, 1990. 158.

"Kathryn Kuhlman, Part Two." *The Pittsburgher.* n.d.

"Kathryn Kuhlman." *Institute for the Study of American Evangelicals.* websource: http://isae.wheaton.edu/hall-of-biography/kathryn-j-kuhlman/; accessed: 1023/2011.

Kathryn Kuhlman Denver revival quotation from Denver Tabernacle. March 10, 1935. *Tabernacle Joy Bells* (courtesy Western History Collection, Denver Public Library).

"Kathryn Kuhlman: Dying to Self." *Christianity Today.* March 12, 1976, v. 20, #12), 47-48.

Kathryn Kuhlman explains why people fall down under the Holy Spirit's influence *God's Generals Website.* accessed 7/29/2011.

Kathryn Kuhlman gives altar call in southern California crusade *God's Generals Website.* accessed 7/29/2011.

Kathryn Kuhlman interviews lady who is healed in the Israel crusade *God's Generals Website.* accessed 7/29/2011.

Kathryn Kuhlman interviews Turkish man healed in the Israel crusade *God's Generals Website.* accessed 7/29/2011.

Kathryn Kuhlman leads worship *God's Generals Website.* accessed 7/29/2011.

Kathryn Kuhlman opens the miracle service in prayer, video, *YouTube.* accessed, 7/29/2011.

Kathryn Kuhlman speaks of a spiritual secret *God's Generals Website.* accessed 7/29/2011.

Kathryn Kuhlman to Mr. Claude Mural McLaughlin (1911–1949). Akron, OH. October 4, 1949, personal letter of encouragement. Kuhlman writes: "I wish so very much that it would be possible for me to step into your home and just speak an encouraging word. That is not possible. Sincerely, I want you to know that your prayer request was received and my personal attention, and with you I am believing God for your healing. 'Fear not for I am with thee. Be not afraid for I am thy God. I will strengthen thee; I will help you,' Isaiah 41:10. Yours in Christ, Kathryn Kuhlman."

Kathryn Kuhlman, Curriculum Vitae. Provide by Carol Gray and the Kathryn Kuhlman Foundation.

Kay, William K. and Dyer, Anne E., eds. *Pentecostal and Charismatic Studies: A Reader.* London: SCM Press, 2004.

Kay, William K., *Pentecostalism, A Very Short Introduction.* New York: Oxford University Press, Inc., 2011.

Kempis, Thomas A., trans. Whitford, Richard. *The Imitation of Christ.* New York: Washington Square Press, Inc. 1964.

King, Marie Gentert, ed. *Foxe's Book of Martyrs.* Old Tappan, NJ: Fleming H. Revell Company, 1972.

Kuhlman, Kathryn. "Blockades That Determine Destiny." *The Latter Rain Evangel.* vol. 28, no. 6, March, 1937): 6-8.

__________. *An Hour with Kathryn Kuhlman.* Audiotape of lecture by Kathryn Kuhlman. Kathryn Kuhlman Foundation.

__________. *Baptism of the Holy Spirit.* Audiotape of lecture by Kathryn Kuhlman. Kathryn Kuhlman Foundation.

__________. *Dry Land...Living Water: Las Vegas Miracle Service.* Produced by the Kathryn Kuhlman Foundation, 1975. Video CD.

__________. *God Can Do It Again.* Old Tappan, NJ: Fleming H. Revell Company, 1974.

__________. *Graduation to Glory, Kathryn Kuhlman at Oral Roberts University.* Produced by Oral Roberts University, Videocassette.

__________. *Heart to Heart.* Vol. I. Alachua, FL: Bridge-Logos, 1983.

__________. *I Believe in Miracles.* New York: Pyramid Books, 1962.

__________. *In Search of Blessings: Sermons on the Beatitudes.* Alachua, FL: Bridge-Logos, 1989.

__________. *In Tribute to Kathryn Kuhlman.* Audiotape presented by the Kathryn Kuhlman Foundation, #488/5054.

__________. *Nothing Is Impossible With God.* Englewood Cliffs, NJ: Prentice-Hall, Inc., 1974.

__________. *Nerves.* Audiotape of lecture by Kathryn Kuhlman presented for radio. Kathryn Kuhlman Foundation. Radio Talks. #3/#4, 1980.

__________. "Soul Burden a Test of Spirituality." *The Latter Rain Evangel.* vol. 28, no. 2, November 1936) 5–11.

__________. with Buckingham, Jamie. *A Glimpse Into Glory.* South Plainfield, NJ: Bridge Publishing, Inc., 1983.

__________. *Quietness Within Ourselves.* Audiotape of lecture by Kathryn Kuhlman presented for radio. Kathryn Kuhlman Foundation. Radio Talks. #597/637, 1978.

Land, Steven Jack. *Pentecostal Spirituality: A Passion for the Kingdom.* Cleveland, TN: CPT Press, 2010) 3.

Lee, Joyce and Gohr, Glenn. "Women In the Pentecostal Movement." *Enrichment Journal.* Assemblies of God USA, Fall 1999. <http://womeninministry.ag.org/history/index.cfm>.

Lee, Norman. "Article On Evangelist Swamps the Journal With Demands For Reprints." *The Allegheny Journal.* Thursday, August 24, 1950.

Lee, Norman. "Kathryn Kuhlman, Hundreds Pray at 'Altar Call for Salvation.'" *The Allegheny Journal.* Thursday, September 7, 1950, 2.

Liardon, Roberts. *God's Generals.* Tulsa, OK: Albury Publishing, 1996.

_______________. *Kathryn Kuhlman: A Spiritual Biography of God's Miracle Working Power.* Tulsa: OK, Harrison House, 1973.

"Local Group Will Go to Pittsburgh to Hear Evangelist." *The Daily Courier.* Connellsville, PA. Thursday, April 28, 1949.

Lucas, Doug. "The Kathryn Kuhlman Story Northside's Most Famous Evangelist." *The Allegheny City Society Reporter Dispatch.* Summer 2006.

Malachuk, Viola. interview by phone 1/29/11. Widow of Dan Malachuk who founded Logos International and organized Kuhlman's Jerusalem events. Viola was a personal friend of Kuhlman and Dan Malachuk was on the board of regents at ORU.

McConnell, D.R. *A Different Gospel: A Historical and Biblical Analysis of the Modern Faith Movement.* Peabody, MA: Hendrickson Publishers, Inc., 1988.

McDougal, Dennis. "Oral Roberts Program May Be Blacked Out Here Sunday." Los Angeles Times, January 16, 1987.

McGinn, Bernard. *The Foundations of Mysticism: Origins to the Fifth Century.* NY: The Crossroad Publishing Company, 1992.

Menzies, William W. Ph.D. *Anointed to Serve, The Story of the Assemblies of God.* Springfield: Gospel Publishing House, 1971.

Meyer Everts, Janet. "Brokenness as the Center of a Woman's Ministry." *Pneuma.* Vol. 17, No. 2, Fall 1995.

"Money for Crippled Children." raised by Kathryn Kuhlman for Old Newsboy's Children's Hospital fundraiser." Nov. 1948.

Moltmann, Jürgen. *The Source: The Holy Spirit and the Theology of Life.* Minneapolis, MN: Fortress Press, 1997.

Moltmann, Jürgen. *The Spirit of Life: A Universal Affirmation.* Minneapolis, MN: Fortress Press, 1992.

Murray, Andrew, Andrew Murray, *With Christ in the School of Prayer.* Springdale, PA: Whitaker House, 1981.

Nicklay, Deb. "Salvation and Scandal," *The Globe Gazette North Iowa Media Group.* posted Sunday, January 28, 2007.

__________. correspondence dated 10/25/2010.

Palmer, Phoebe. *Faith and Its Effects: How to Receive the Blessing of a Sanctified Life.* Salem, OH: Schmul Publishing Co., 1999.

Palmer, Phoebe *Full Salvation.* Salem OH: n.d..

Palmer, Phoebe. *Entire Devotion to God.* Salem, OH: Schmul Publishing Co., Inc., n.d..

Palmer, Phoebe. *The Way of Holiness: Notes By the Way.* Salem, OH: Schmul Publishing Co., Inc., n.d..

Photo of Denver Revival Tabernacle with large letters "Evangelist Kathryn Kuhlman" on side of large, plain warehouse. A large sign rises over building: "Prayer Changes Things." websource: http://4bp.blogspot.com/ accessed 1/8/2011.

Photo of Tink Wilkerson c. 1960s at his auto dealership courtesy of the Beryl Ford Collection/Rotary Club of Tulsa.

Photo of Wilkerson's Chevrolet Auto Dealership, 705 South Boulder, Tulsa 3, Oklahoma.

"Rev. Parrott Will Open Revival Campaign Here: First Meeting Sunday, 200 voices, 50-Piece Orchestra, To Assist at All Services." *newspaper article.* n.d.

R. Marie Griffith, review of *Kathryn Kuhlman: The Woman Behind the Miracles.* by Wayne E. Warner. *Pneuma: The Journal of the Society for Pentecostal Studies.* vol. 19, No. 2, Fall 1997, 274-276.

"Roberts Not Counting on Hospital Miracle." *The Los Angeles Times,* September 16, 1989, AP. websource: http://articles.latimes.com/keyword/city-of-faith-hospital. accessed 2/26/2011. "Tulsa Car Dealers." *TulsaTVMemories.com*; websource: http://tulsatvmemories.com/cars.html; accessed 10/23/10; D.B. Wilkerson, the retired owner of Wilkerson Chevrolet Inc., died Monday. He was 88. Wilkerson was born on May 24, 1912, in Fort Smith, Ark. He graduated from high school in Fort Smith in 1930 and began his automotive career as an employee of Adams Motor Co. In 1932, he purchased a parking lot, where he operated a used car business until he received a Chevrolet franchise in 1954. Wilkerson was elected to the board of directors of Major Engineering Co. in 1966. In 1972, he received a Quality Dealer Award from Time magazine. Wilkerson played a major role in the development of Oral Roberts University and received an honorary doctorate in 1980 for his commitment to the American free enterprise system and for his support of ORU. He is survived by two daughters, Marilyn Olsson of Tulsa and Dianne Lewallen of Plano, Texas; one son, D.B. "Tink" Wilkerson Jr. of Tulsa; eight grandchildren; and 14 great-grandchildren.

Roberts, Oral. *The Call: Oral Roberts Autobiography.* Old Tappan, NJ: Fleming H. Revell Company, 1971.

Rogers, Darrin J. "Bringing History to You," *AG Heritage.* 2008, 3: One of the acquisitions of the at the Flower Pentecostal Heritage Center in 2007 was three notebooks of Kathryn Kuhlman sermon transcriptions, donated by Patricia Pickard.

Schwarz, Gerry to Burroughs Waltrip, Jr., letter from dated July 6, 2004, archived in the Flower Pentecostal Heritage Center Collections, The Assemblies of God Headquarters, Springfield, MO. Schwarz was an English instructor at North Iowa Area Community College, who wrote articles about Waltrip and the Radio Chapel.

__________. "Burroughs A. Waltrip and the Radio Chapel." unpublished story collection, 7/6/2004.

__________. correspondence dated 1/28/2011.

Simpson, Charles, Baker. "Making Disciples." *New Wine Magazine.* Vol. 6, No. 3, March 1974: 4-8.

Spraggett, Allen. *Kathryn Kuhlman, The Woman Who Believed in Miracles.* New York: The American Library, Inc., 1970.

__________. *The Unexplained, Startling new discoveries in ESP by a leading expert.* New York: The American Library, Inc., 1967.

Synan, Vinson. "A Healer in the House? A Historical Perspective on Healing in the Pentecostal/Charismatic Tradition." *AJPS* 3/2. 2000: 189-201.

Tinlin, Paul B., and Blumhofer, Edith L. "Decade of Decline or Harvest? Dilemmas of the Assemblies of God, *The Christian Century.* October 1991.

"To Hear K. Kuhlman, A special street car will be operated…in order to accommodate people in the community who desire to hear Kathryn Kuhlman." *The Daily Courier, Connellsville, PA.* Wednesday, May 24, 1950.

"To Lead Revival Services." "Burroughs A. Waltrip will conduct daily revival services at the People's Gospel Tabernacle this week," and "Evangelists Will Conduct Services Here: Burroughs A. Waltrips and his wife, Kathryn Kuhlman Waltrip, will conduct a series of revival services at People's Gospel Tabernacle commencing Sunday at 9 a.m." *The Lima News. Ohio.* Oct. 8, 1939.

Transcribed notes taken at various Kuhlman services from 1949 to 1952; Flower Pentecostal Heritage Center collection.

Wacker, Grant. *Heaven Below: Early Pentecostals and American Culture.* Cambridge, MA: Harvard University Press, 2001.

"Walks at Service: Richard Burger of Akron, Ohio, has been paralyzed since he was 4 years of age. He is shown above as he walked, through the aisles during Kathryn Kuhlman service held at Faith Temple in Franklin, PA, on Sunday, August 27." *The Allegheny Journal.* Thursday, September 7, 1950.

Waltrip, Jr., Burroughs, correction written for an online article dated 7/22/2002.

__________. correspondence dated 1/14/2011; 1/22/2011, response to questions; 1/24/2011, 12/22/2011.

__________. to Gerry Schwarz letter dated June 28, 2004.

Warrington, Keith, *Pentecostal Theology: A Theology of Encounter.* London: T&T Clark, 2008.

Warner, Wayne E. "At the Grass-Roots: Kathryn Kuhlman's Pentecostal-Charismatic Influence on Historic Mainstream Churches," *Pneuma: The Journal of the Society for Pentecostal Studies.* Vol. 17., No. 1, Spring 1995: 51-65.

__________. *Kathryn Kuhlman, the Woman Behind the Miracles.* Ann Arbor, MI: Servant Publications, 1993.

Warner, Wayne E., correspondence, dated: 3/22/2011, 3/26/2011, 4/1/2011, 8/13/2011.

Yong, Amos. *The Spirit Poured Out on All Flesh, Pentecostalism and the Possibility of Global Theology.* Grand Rapids, MI: Baker Academic, 2005.

Young, Frances M. *Brokenness & Blessing, Towards a Biblical Spirituality.* Grand Rapids: Baker, 2007.